Beethoven
or Bust

Beethoven
or Bust

▼

A Practical Guide to Understanding and Listening to Great Music

David Hurwitz

ANCHOR BOOKS
DOUBLEDAY
NEW YORK LONDON TORONTO SYDNEY AUCKLAND

AN ANCHOR BOOK
PUBLISHED BY DOUBLEDAY
a division of Bantam Doubleday Dell Publishing Group, Inc.
666 Fifth Avenue, New York, New York 10103

ANCHOR BOOKS, DOUBLEDAY, and the portrayal of an anchor
are trademarks of Doubleday, a division of Bantam
Doubleday Dell Publishing Group, Inc.

BOOK DESIGN BY TASHA HALL

Library of Congress Cataloging-in-Publication Data
Hurwitz, David, 1961–
  Beethoven or bust : a practical guide to understanding
and listening to great music / David Hurwitz.
      p.   cm.
  Includes index.
  1. Music appreciation. II. Title.
MT6.H887B4   1992
781.6'8—dc20   91-35677
                                                          CIP
                                                          MN

ISBN 0-385-42054-4

ALL RIGHTS RESERVED
PRINTED IN THE UNITED STATES OF AMERICA
May 1992
10 9 8 7 6 5 4 3 2 1
FIRST EDITION

To my brother Dan for getting me started,
and my sister Jodie who was right all along,
with love and affection

Acknowledgments

The elements of music are few, and their combinations many. So it is also with writing, especially about music. Anyone who has read some of the great musical scholars of our century, Donald Francis Tovey and Charles Rosen in particular, will find familiar things here, and I can only hope that my understanding of them doesn't do them an injustice. I also must acknowledge a debt to Richard Dawkins, whose stimulating book on evolution, *The Blind Watchmaker,* contains an argument on the nature of human complexity that helped to clarify my own thoughts on the matter. Finally, I must list all those wonderful friends without whose support and criticism this project would never have made it into your living room. You have them to blame as much as me: Chaim Roitgrund, Bill Harkins, Remy Farkas, the gang at Recordmasters in Baltimore, Paul Wakabayashi, Carol Brown, Patricia Reilly, Ted Libbey, Vernon Lidtke, James Bucar, John Smith, Lowell Halvorson, Daniella, Mignon, and Arthur Reik, Meta Brophy, Israel and Amy Rodriguez, Deirdre Hudson, Jon Red, Leo Pagarigan, Joel Press, Sheila Leonard, Barry Guerrero, Inge Kjemtrup, Carl Schuster, Steve Miller, Harvey Allen, Jeff Blum, Howard Bourdages, Andy Nelson, Irene and Leanna Chamish, Bill Poole, Kitty and Dave Merrihew, Barbara Perry, Deborah Federoff, Paul Schlitz, Irene Miller, Annette Aguilar, Izzy Miranda, Louis and Moshe Kestenbaum, Nate Plafker, and my wonderful parents.

Table of Contents

Introduction   1

Part I: Mastering the Language

1 ▼ Classical Music?   7

2 ▼ Record Buying   12

3 ▼ Understanding the Orchestra: The Baroque—
      Why Use Instruments?   21

4 ▼ Understanding the Orchestra: The Sonata
      Orchestra   35

5 ▼ Forms and Patterns: How Is Music
      Organized?   46

6 ▼ Musical Memory: Training the Ear to
      Recognize Musical Ideas   67

7 ▼ Large Forms in Small Packages:
      Chamber Music   76

8 ▼ Solo Personalities: The Concerto   94

9 ▼ Musical Description: Program Music   106

10 ▼ Musical Meaning: The Three Basic Kinds of
      Musical Expression   116

Part II: The Master's Voice

Introduction   129

Listening Groups 1–88   132

Glossary   213

Index of Musical Compositions   221

Introduction

BEFORE MAN DISCOVERED FIRE, LIFE WAS relatively uncomplicated. If he was hungry, he killed something and ate it raw. When he felt cold, he wrapped himself in animal skins. But we're civilized now. We cook our meat and wear polyester. All of us, that is, except a tiny minority, which spends huge sums of money, eats raw hamburger and wraps itself in animal skins—often as a prelude to a genteel evening at the opera, theater, or symphony.

When I was in college, the campus concert series was the territorial preserve of one of these neo-Neanderthals. As director of classical programming at the student radio station, I thought it would be a good idea to promote the concerts by giving away a few tickets on the air. It wasn't as if the performances ever sold out or anything. But my pleas were unavailing. The aforementioned benefactress of the series regarded me with that singular distaste usually reserved for representatives of the Unwashed Masses, and said, "People should have to pay for art. If they can't afford it, then they don't deserve it."

With those words, the idea for this book was born. I'd like to return the great classics of music to the people for whom they were written—you and me. Basically, I'm just a banker and an all-around music nut. I don't know if this qualifies me to write a book about music, but since I've gone and done it anyway, I'll have to live with the consequences of my indiscretion. I don't think I'm displaying any false modesty when I say that this is probably the best book on music written by a banker that you'll ever read. To that extent, it's self-recommending.

This is a book about music and, more important, about thinking musically. There are no little biographies of composers, no lectures on comparative culture, no charts and graphs, and no examples that require you to read music. My entire premise is a simple one: music occurs in time, not on paper. Therefore, the only significant concern is *what you actually hear.* This in turn depends on how good a listener you are, and what you're listening to. The two parts of this book address these two issues. Part One systematically (and I hope painlessly) helps you to understand the principles of musical form, and trains your musical memory. Part Two is a sort of musical Rosetta stone: a series of comparisons based on easily audible musical ideas that help you follow your own interests even as you hear the language of music at work.

Make no mistake about it: music is a language. The purveyors of "music appreciation" claim that the best way to understand this language is to study its environment. They teach you about the instruments of the orchestra, the history of musical notation, the lives of the composers, and the historical factors that led to the creation of each musical work. Then they show you a painting or read a poem from the same period, play the music, and say, "Now, isn't that perfectly clear?" I suppose that this is one way to approach the subject. But if we think of music as a language, then it becomes obvious just how crooked this path actually is. Imagine that you wanted to learn Chinese, and your teacher told you that all you had to do was study the life of Chairman Mao, see the Great Wall, buy a Ming dynasty vase, eat at a Chinese restaurant, and drink tea. See what I'm getting at?

The best way to learn any language is the usual way. You

study grammar, syntax, pronunciation, and you *listen* to native speakers. With music, which speaks of emotion and feeling on a nonverbal level, all you have to do is spend enough time with it and you'll pick it up. But you can't do that in a classroom, in one semester, while fretting about a final grade. The process takes years, and is itself one of music's great rewards. Even so, there's much to enjoy immediately, and your pleasure will increase on repetition as you discover depths unrevealed the first time around.

How then do you use this book to become a better listener? Well, that's more or less up to you. The important thing is to *keep listening.* Ideally, you should probably work on Parts One and Two simultaneously. But if you're really a beginner, then start here and read at least the first four chapters of Part One. The two parts are heavily interconnected, both by composers and specific compositions. So if you hear a work that you like in Part One, use it or the composer as a springboard into Part Two.

The body of musical literature is vast. I've concentrated on orchestral and chamber music because it's what most people listen to at first. But Part Two contains a good amount of vocal music, and even a few operas. It's both impossible and unwise to segregate music too specifically. Variety and contrast give our musical tradition depth and meaning. But some choices have to be made, and I think I've struck a reasonable compromise.

Many of the composers you will encounter in these pages may be unfamiliar to you. That's only natural. The main peril in getting to know our musical heritage is the ever present threat of falling into a bottomless pit. By the same token there's much more to Western music than Bach, Mozart, Beethoven, and Brahms. Who's to say what music suits you best? Keep your ears open. Listen to the radio. Best of all, work through this book with a friend. Split the cost of acquiring recordings, go to concerts, listen together, and talk about what you've heard. You may respond to Sibelius and dislike Beethoven. That's perfectly all right, so long as you permit yourself to grow into the works you might not enjoy at first. I've never understood why we so often feel the need to despise ten things for every one that we accept. All of the music discussed in this book is worth your time, but you have to set your own priorities. That first step will be the most difficult.

This book presupposes your starting a record collection, and therefore making a serious financial investment. I think that this is an advantage because unless you're rich, you'll have to take lots of time getting started. You should resist the temptation to progress too quickly. Listen to your new acquisitions several times, come to know each piece inside out, and then move on. I have tried to make things a little more economical by selecting works that I know come coupled on recordings. But I can't vouch for the longevity of anything in the catalogue. I don't think any of my points depend on music that is especially hard to get, but I have included a chapter on record buying which should help cope with any problems that might arise.

Music has always been part of my life. It's hard for me to imagine being without it. My approach to the topic is admittedly subjective, which means that you should feel free to disagree with me. In fact, forming your own opinions and developing your own taste for music are much more important than any of my personal cultural preoccupations. The essence of listening lies in striking a delicate balance between keeping as open a mind as possible, while fearlessly employing—and learning to trust—your powers of judgment.

Part I

▼

Mastering the Language

1

▼

Classical Music?

NOT TOO LONG AGO, I WAS WAITING FOR a subway. Across the platform, a man was playing an amplified harmonica. The noise was deafening, and no one seemed much inclined to toss him any money for his efforts. Suddenly, he struck up the "Ode to Joy" from Beethoven's Ninth Symphony. I watched amazed as the people on the platform began tossing coins into his cup. It was an impressive demonstration of the power of classical music, even under the most adverse of circumstances.

Classical music pervades our lives, and you would probably be amazed at how much you know without realizing it. General Electric seductively underlines the soft whiteness of their light bulbs to the mellow strains of Pachelbel's *Canon*, while Dodge pickups haul themselves over the rough terrain of Mussorgsky's *Night on Bald Mountain*. If Madison Avenue offers any indication, classical music has come of age. More and more people are buying records, tapes, and especially compact discs, and discovering that orchestral music best demonstrates superior recording technology.

Unfortunately, however, the world of classical music can be a difficult one to enter. This is not really the fault of the music. After all, what composers would not want their works to be popular? Rather, the problem lies with the social and cultural environments within which we encounter the great classics of music. And there is economic reality too. As both our harmonica player and our advertisers know, any music is valued, at least in part, by its ability either directly or indirectly to bring in the bucks. And classical music has never been as profitable to the record companies as pop. So as long as the often prohibitive price of and lack of access to decent concert seats make recordings the principal source of our musical culture, record company executives, advertisers, and sponsors will be the powers governing our musical lives.

Rather than bemoaning this state of affairs, let us take advantage of it. The music industry, fortunately, seems to have decided that the classics can indeed earn their keep, and it has invested enormous sums of money in new technologies that especially benefit orchestral and "acoustic" music of all sorts. Public response has far surpassed expectations. People everywhere have discovered that classical music is an excellent accompaniment for jogging, reading, driving, sex, insomnia, childbirth, house plants, and heaven knows what else. It's also great for listening. But so many have perceived the beauty of great music, only to be put off by the bewildering number of recordings, the volume of repertoire, and the snobbish condescension of local enthusiasts and patrons of the arts.

This book attempts to make some sense out of the confusion. It will help you to help yourself discover the fun and pleasure in *really* listening to music. Note the omission of the word "classical." When we speak of classical music, we commonly mean something like a symphony or an opera. But what about a Broadway musical, or the Beatles? How about John Williams' music to *Star Wars*? Let's begin by answering these questions with a quick look at our musical tradition.

Take three pieces of music from different periods: a Gregorian chant, Beethoven's Fifth Symphony, and *Ionization* by Edgard Varèse. You've probably heard Gregorian chants. They were set down during the Middle Ages, but can still be heard during most Catholic masses, or behind any television commercial featuring monks. Usually sung by unaccompanied male voices, they consist entirely of a Latin religious text set to a single line of melody. Beethoven's Fifth is probably the best-known classical work ever written. The symphony requires an orchestra containing one piccolo, pairs of flutes, clarinets, oboes, bassoons, trumpets, and horns, one contrabassoon, three trombones, timpani, and the usual five-part string section of first and second violins, violas, cellos, and basses. *Ionization* you have probably not heard. It is a brief piece written for thirteen solo percussionists, and has scarcely any definite notes at all. Varèse published *Ionization* in 1934, well over a century after Beethoven wrote his Fifth, and around a thousand years after the compilation of Gregorian chant. Most sensible people would admit that all three items fall into the category of classical music.

So, if this is classical music, then what do these pieces have in common? The answer, I hope unsurprisingly, is "virtually nothing." Classical music is not a *style* or a *medium,* but rather an estimation of *worth* as determined by the ability of the listener to respond to, understand, and enjoy the music over time. When enough people continue to demand the same piece for long enough it becomes a classic, whether it is a symphony, song, musical, opera, or anything else. Unfortunately, no one has figured out the length of time it takes for something to become a classic. This depends on a number of factors, including frequency of performance, popularity, and presumably the quality of the work in question.

Actually, the mass availability of recordings, which perpetuate music indefinitely, has radically redefined the process by which music becomes classical. The number of musical works, both old and new, that can be accommodated by recording approaches the infinite. When all that really matters is your personal preference, it's pointless to worry about why some things are classical and others are not. On the other hand, it's perfectly reasonable to want to enjoy the thousand or so years of terrific music waiting for your discovery.

So, philosophically, it may be a waste of time to distinguish between classical and nonclassical music. But this is reality, and we all know what we generally mean by the term: Gregorian chant,

Beethoven's Fifth, and just about anything else that is not a song written in the last few years. And there *are* valid reasons why you may find these generally acknowledged classics difficult to take in at first sitting.

The biggest problem in approaching music in extended forms, such as symphonies and concertos, is the fact that we are not taught to listen intently on a large time-scale. Just compare the way we listen with the way we use our eyes. Let's say our sense of sight has two components: the practical and the aesthetic. The practical use of vision is obvious; we must recognize things and see where we are going. The aesthetic component receives rigorous training from birth. We look at pictures, decorate our rooms, coordinate our wardrobes, draw, watch television, and everywhere observe and learn the possibilities of combining colors and images into various patterns.

Hearing also has practical and aesthetic elements. The practical side of our auditory sense permits us to receive information in the form of meaningful noise, whether verbal or nonverbal, as with a siren. But music, one of the most significant aesthetic aspects of hearing, does not get the same sort of comprehensive attention given the everyday use of sight. The music we encounter daily usually comes in the form of songs, which are by definition short and generally very simple. Anything longer than five or six minutes gets classified as background music, which we either tune out or use to accompany some other primary task. The real problem, then, has nothing to do with classical versus nonclassical music, but rather with small- and large-scale art forms, and the attention we give them. A song by Schubert has more in common with a song by Led Zeppelin than it does with a Beethoven symphony, even though Beethoven and Schubert were contemporaries. Why then, do we find a symphony so imposingly difficult? Let's carry our analogy a bit further and find out.

Sight is an almost instantaneous phenomenon. The differences between a line drawing and the *Mona Lisa* are enormous, but they take only a moment to register, and you have a lifetime of associated images stored up that tell you whether or not the picture deserves another look. And it doesn't necessarily take longer to look at bigger pictures, or works done in different styles. But in music, big means long. The nearest visual equivalent to a great symphony might be a flight over the Grand Canyon or a tour of Buckingham Palace—something that takes time to see in the same way that music takes time to hear. A book like this can only try to hasten the process of understanding by suggesting situations in which your time will be put to the best use.

Finally, forget about the idea that classical music is supposed to be so difficult and complex that it can only be enjoyed after deep and serious study. Like all great art, the musical classics *reward* deep and serious study, but this is hardly a prerequisite. In fact, in the days before recording, composers had to be extra sure that new pieces made their impression immediately, because another performance might never occur. The only advantage those audiences had over you was that they had enough time on their hands to have had a greater exposure to large-scale music. Really that was, and is, the only significant difference; and they had nowhere near the abundant choice that modern recordings offer you.

Music comes in many different forms. Up to this point, your principal exposure has probably been to one basic type—the song. But a vast treasure house of larger forms awaits your notice. The reason that the great classics offer the best beginning to your musical journey is simply that the great composers spoke the language of music better than anyone else. Their work, aside from being terrifically entertaining and enjoyable in its own right, will show you how to enjoy any kind of music at all, because it will reveal the meaning of musical speech to you. It's only a matter of time, and attention. Let the music do the rest.

2

▼

Record Buying

THE VAST ARRAY OF CLASSICAL RECORDINGS available for purchase can be even more bewildering than the music itself. Nevertheless, the process of starting to really enjoy music of any kind these days virtually presupposes building a record collection. This is especially desirable when the music so consistently rewards repeated listening. This chapter offers a practical guide to classical record labels, prices, and recording mediums. It is very easy to assemble an excellent collection at relatively small cost. Here's how.

LABELS

It would be a monumental task to survey every record label individually, especially in such a traditionally unstable and badly managed industry. Instead, it's better to get a sense of how the major labels organize their catalogues. To begin with, most companies offer their product at three price levels: budget, mid-price, and full price. Some labels devote themselves to specific areas of the repertoire, but most try to maintain a comprehensive general catalogue of the "meat and potatoes" classics—Bach, Beethoven, Brahms, Mozart, and so on—often at all three price levels. But don't think that a full-price record assures better quality in either performance or sound. In fact, the opposite is often the case.

The actual choice of recorded repertoire reflects a compromise between what the artist wants to record, and what the record company thinks its catalogue needs. Virtually all new recordings are issued at full price, and this forces older (and often better) recordings of the same piece down in the price structure. Because classical recordings are so costly and expected sales so small, record companies find it profitable to keep older performances in print at lower price levels to help offset the cost of new productions. And often, they support the "serious" side of recording by issuing crossover discs. These generally involve either classical artists singing or playing pop music (Pavarotti sings "Twisted Sister"), or pop artists performing the classics (Julio Iglesias sings Wagner). However weird the premise, these albums invariably make heaps of money and are never less than entertaining, if often in unexpected ways.

As you get to know the various labels, you will notice that record companies build their catalogues around a certain stable of performers. Many of these artists record the same repertoire more than once as the years go by, increasingly complicating the matter of choice. Always remember that the latest go-round is by no means necessarily the best. Also, although it might be easier to get complete sets of, for example, the Beethoven symphonies, it is usually better to resist this temptation. Keep in mind that a performer's art is not essentially creative, but re-creative. Many artists satisfy their vanity by recording areas of the repertoire for which they have no affinity. So try to experience the range of interpretation offered by different performers, for this will reveal the many facets of the music better than any single interpretive viewpoint.

RECORDS, TAPES, AND COMPACT DISCS

By far the greatest innovation to hit the record industry has been the compact disc (CD), along with the advent of digital recording techniques. These make possible greatly improved sound reproduction—at least potentially. Do not get suckered in by the word "digital" on a recording. The most important factors in recording acoustical music of any kind are recording locale and microphone placement. Many of the best-sounding compact discs actually represent transfers of much older, nondigital (analogue) material.

CDs have practically eliminated the market for vinyl LPs, at least in the world of classical music. Record companies have stopped producing LPs in all but exceptional cases. Cassettes remain popular, both for use in cars and portable tape decks, and because manufacturers offer extra-length compilations at very low prices. Of course, tapes wear out in time, a problem that will also afflict digital audio tape (DAT) or any other recordable, impermanent medium. The good news is that because CDs are available at all price levels, the real cost of building a record collection remains substantially the same as in the days of LPs, and CD players cost far less than an audiophile quality turntable.

CHOOSING A RECORDING

The single most important piece of information in choosing a recording is the name of the piece that you want to buy. In the case of something like Mussorgsky's *Pictures at an Exhibition,* this requirement is easily met. But many of the more prolific composers wrote several pieces of the same type: Vivaldi's concertos, for example, number in the hundreds. In this case, there are other ways of making sure that you are actually getting what you want.

Like the public, composers (and their publishers) needed a system that would keep track of their music. The generally agreed-upon answer to this requirement was the *opus number*. "Opus" is Latin for "work" (the plural is "opera," usually abbreviated "Opp."), and many composers and publishers simply kept a numerical list of their works. For example, Beethoven's Fifth Symphony is his Opus 67, and nothing else by him has that number. Thus, the full title of the piece is Symphony No. 5 in C minor, Op. 67. Here no problem could arise, since Beethoven only wrote one Fifth Symphony—indeed, only one symphony in the key of C minor. So any of the three pieces of information contained in the full title would be sufficient. But take the case of a Haydn string quartet in C major. Haydn wrote some sixty-eight string quartets, and several are in that key. So here an opus number is essential: String Quartet in C major, Op. 74, No. 1. Why No. 1? Because this particular opus consists of three complete quartets grouped together, each of which has a number within the opus designation.

Unfortunately, the laws of fashion that determine which composers are in style, the unscrupulousness of publishers, and several wars and other upheavals have not made the job of organizing a composer's output easy. Many works were not published during their composer's lifetime, and so other systems had to be used. Just resign yourself to making a note of these as you go along. For example, in the case of Haydn, at least four different systems are in use. The symphonies are numbered consecutively (though not entirely chronologically), 1 through 104, with two other symphonies called "A" and "B" discovered after the initial batch. The string quartets have opus numbers (but some of the earliest of these seem not to have been written by Haydn at all). As for everything else, there are assorted systems named after the organization or person who put the organizing catalogue together.

Actually it is not necessary to go too far into this mess. To save your sanity, I have put together a quick list of the most important alternative systems and the composers whose music they catalogue.

Mozart. Mozart has "K" numbers, which stand for Köchel, the guy who put together the definitive list of Mozart's works (well after his death). A typical sample: Symphony No. 40 in G minor, K. 550. Note, however, that the symphony is also numbered, this being the more common designation.

Bach. Bach has "BWV" numbers, which stand in this case for the catalogue of his works, assembled over time by a number of editors working for a scholarly society dedicated to this purpose.

Vivaldi. Vivaldi has "RV" numbers, which are analogous to Mozart's "Ks," but some of his best-known works have opus numbers as well. And remember, posterity long ago recognized the difficulty, and gave titles to very popular pieces. So in the case of Vivaldi's *The Four Seasons,* technically part of his Twelve Violin Concertos, Op. 8, you needn't worry about any of this.

Schubert. Schubert has "D" numbers, which stand for Deutsch, who did for Schubert what Köchel did for Mozart.

These four are the most important exceptions to the opus system of cataloguing, and you probably won't have to deal with them that often. It's useful, however, to know what's going on. I often think that if the people responsible for making the catalogues had any sense of humility at all, they would have stuck with opus numbers. That way, the few who remembered their hard work would at least do so with fondness instead of exasperation.

REVIEWS

People seem to trust the printed word, a fact that has its good and bad sides. In the case of record reviews, a healthy skepticism should prevail (unless, of course, I'm the author, in which case you may accept my advice as Divine Revelation). The criteria of music criticism are so subjective and personal that no single performance has ever received unanimous praise. Also, whatever the disillusioned might say, the general caliber of recorded performance these days is rather high. You most likely will not buy anything positively awful. But a bad performance is a dull performance, more often than not, and a new musical experience should be stimulating at least. So reviews do have a place.

The best critiques take into account comparisons with other recordings of the same work, pointing out differences in performance, price, technical quality, and presentation. Remember that knowing music and knowing recordings are not exactly synonymous, and if critics say something is bad, they should also let you know what's good. Otherwise, the best way to record shop is the old-fashioned way—through word of mouth. Find a friend or salesclerk you trust and let that person guide you. You'll develop ideas of your own in no time at all. If you do read reviews, look for the warning signs that tell you when to get suspicious. You should take with a grain of salt any reviewers who:

1.   Don't like the music they're reviewing (as opposed to the performance in question)

2.   Refer to anyone connected with the recording—conductor, soloist, producer, recording engineer—as a personal acquaintance

3.   Reject the entire interpretive approach as illegitimate, and/or

4.   Talk only about the sound or the performance, but not both

IN THE STORE

Whatever you read, keep in mind that most review publications only deal with new releases, and these are seldom the preferred performances of the piece in question. Hence the importance of comparative reviews, which generally tell you what's the best of the lot in the critic's eyes. You can of course bypass the entire review business if you simply ask for assistance from the classics salesperson (assuming there is one) in your local record store. Most of these people will be eager to help you, though many forget all too quickly that they were once starting out as well. If a recording is out of stock, most stores will order it for you, though this works better with the smaller shops than with big chains. You can do a lot to help yourself, however, if you follow some simple rules:

1.   Check the album or ask about recording dates. This is very important for two reasons. First, anything recorded in the last thirty-five years or so will probably be sonically acceptable if not necessarily outstanding. Second, although many wonderful "historical" recordings by very great musicians exist, they are not the best way to get acquainted with a work. You are much better off with a decent performance recorded in good sound than with a great performance in horrible sound. There is no such thing as a definitive performance, and only people familiar with many versions of the same work even begin to care about such distinctions. Don't ever let anyone persuade you that you need to sacrifice sound for performance quality.

2.   Find out about return privileges. You will not be allowed to return a recording you do not like. It must be defective. Of course, you can easily "arrange" a defect, but most record stores wisely insist, for just such circumstances, that you exchange the bad copy for one of the same item. If you do get a dud, bring it back immediately.

3.   If you hear something on the radio that you want to buy, write down as much information as possible, keeping in mind the importance of identifying the piece properly, as we have already discussed. If you can't remember any performance details, the opus (or "K" or "D," etc.) number will at least guarantee that you get the right piece. If you are driving or jogging and can't write, then make a mental note of the time that you heard the work in question and call the radio station as soon as possible. They are required by law (and common sense) to keep a log of everything that they play. They will be happy to help you.

4.   Read liner notes. Most recordings come with a set of notes commissioned for the recording. Though seldom extensive, they may help you get to know the music. If the piece is a vocal work, make sure that the text is included. If it's missing, return the recording. If you're in doubt, then ask.

5.   Do not ask to have an open copy played for you. If everyone did this, the result would be chaos. If the salesperson offers, then it's a different story.

6.   If you're buying music of the Baroque or Classical period (Vivaldi, Bach, Handel, Haydn, Mozart, Beethoven— roughly 1600–1830 or so), beware of performances marked "On Original Instruments." Musical scholarship has created a wave of performing ensembles that play on authentic instruments of the period in question, or on modern reproductions. They can sound very different from what you might

expect. Strings are harsher and fewer in number, woodwinds more prominent. The brass instruments lack valves and everything may sound slightly out of tune. On the other hand, you can often hear more detail, the rhythm tends to be springier, and the whole texture sounds more "alive." Generally, this approach works best with Baroque music, the results with Haydn, Mozart, Beethoven, and later music being more controversial. When faced with this kind of choice, do ask to hear a sample of the *kind* of sound involved. Do not let an original-instrument fanatic (yes, they exist) convince you that this is the only way to hear the music. Listen, and decide for yourself.

7.   Take your time and browse. It's absolutely amazing how much quick information you can pick up just by looking at what's available and talking to salespeople and other shoppers. Everyone likes to share a hobby.

8.   If you do not live near a record store that carries classical music, many of the larger ones accept mail or phone orders. You can find these stores in review magazines, especially *Gramophone* and *Fanfare*.

It should be clear by now that knowing music and knowing recordings are two related but differing areas of expertise. You now know something about how to shop for records, and it's time to focus our attention on our primary subject: the music itself.

3

Understanding the Orchestra:
The Baroque—Why Use Instruments?

THE TITLE OF THIS CHAPTER IMPLIES THAT, aside from discovering what an orchestra is, we will also discuss some of the reasons that motivated composers to use instruments for musical expression. As you will see, this point is by no means as obvious as it may sound. But first, we must be quite clear in our intentions when we talk about "understanding" the orchestra.

In the first chapter, I mentioned some of the cultural barriers that render classical music inaccessible to the general public. Once you've recognized that all you need is time, and having seen the snobbery of the cultural elite for the nonsense that it is, the only brake on your ability to listen will be your own perceptions and biases about the comprehensibility of music as art. So let's begin by setting up a mental framework that will dispel some fallacies about art in general, and allow you to think about music constructively.

You may at various times have heard assorted attempts to define art. Such definitions usually sound like: "Art is anything in which the whole is greater than the sum of its parts." Often this implies that art exists in some indefinable spiritual dimension which, in its power to move us emotionally, places it beyond mere mortal understanding. I am convinced that this view is ultimately harmful. Thinking about art this way makes serious rational investigation futile, because art itself remains fundamentally irrational and incomprehensible. Examination of the parts will never—indeed, *can* never—lead us to comprehension of the whole. Thus swathed in mystery, art becomes the special province of the true believer and an intimidating bore to everyone else.

If we take the opposite view, and regard art as precisely the sum of its parts, we can say that examining them does lead to understanding the whole. We have only to see how the interaction of the components creates unity. Interaction is the key. For example, think about building something—like a sailboat. It's not enough to identify the individual pieces. You must know how they fit, and function, together. The reverse also holds true. If you see a sail catch the wind and propel the boat, then you can deduce both the sail's and the boat's purpose. A slack sail hanging in a garage separated from the rest of the boat tells you very little about what it's supposed to do, as does the vessel itself stored upside down in dry dock for the winter.

If we apply the same reasoning to art, we see that art is not a thing, but a process. You can't stop music in time and take it to pieces. The parts only make sense while they're all working together and your attention is engaged by one or more elements within the context of the entire composition. In artistic terms, we would say that form and content are inseparable; what an artist wants to say cannot meaningfully be distinguished from the way he says it. But this does not mean that studying various parts in order to comprehend the whole is worthless. If we pursue our sailboat analogy a bit further, you'll see why.

It may be that pieces of a sailboat are useless alone as a means of transportation, but can't they be assembled in different ways? What would happen, for instance, if you attached the mast and sail to the bottom of the boat? It might float. It might catch the Gulf Stream and get you up to Greenland—eventually. I think we can all agree, however, that this arrangement would be nowhere near as efficient as the correct design.

Now take something more complex, like a computer. Its components can be hooked up in innumerable patterns, but only one will actually work. This brings up an important idea. The more complex the object, the less chance there is that any arrangement of its parts other than the optimal one will produce workable results. Therefore, in any great work of art, substantial alteration of the relationships between its various elements would be inconceivable. Just imagine the *Mona Lisa* with a frown, or consider the shock value of that great lady with her famous mustache and Vandyke. In fact, the complexity of art is the complexity of the human organism, since it represents the deepest and most comprehensive expression of ourselves. The seemingly mystical awe that moves us when we encounter art is nothing less than the miracle and beauty of our own existence captured in all of its wondrous variety. The art itself remains perfectly clear, even though its message can be, and often is, mysterious indeed.

At this point you might justifiably wonder whether it makes any sense to substitute a theory of artistic complexity for one of artistic irrationality. After all, aren't they both equally difficult and intimidating? I don't think so, and if you stay with me for just a minute longer, I can explain why.

People understandably tend to shy away from things they find unduly complicated. Art is no exception. It's much easier to join the cultural elite and claim to be one of the chosen few blessed with the inner light of artistic understanding. Besides, the social benefits surely outweigh the necessary tedium of actually listening! Such people take the question of complexity out of context, ignoring the even larger issue of *purpose*. You don't have to know how to build a sailboat to use one as a means of transportation or sport. Although a computer may be a very complex piece of electronics, its purpose is actually to make your life simpler—*less* complicated. So it is with art. You don't have to know how to write a symphony to listen to one. The complex interactions between the musical elements articulate and express what you as a participant in the artistic experience should perceive. In other words, all of this complexity has one goal: *comprehension.*

So you see, it's not as bad as it sounds. The important thing is to have confidence in your ultimate ability to understand. Why? Because some of the words and music that follow this chapter may not make sense to you at first. You will have to practice listening, and train your mind to respond to musical language. But believe me when I say that in time you will understand, not because of my literary skill, but because composers work so hard to master the complexity of human life and render it comprehensible to us. Trust them.

And now, after this lengthy prelude, we've finally arrived at the orchestra. You should at last be prepared for your musical voyage, because the orchestra will be your sailboat. By learning your way about the orchestra, you will be able to pilot yourself to any point in the musical universe. Understanding what an orchestra is, why it is, and what it does will initiate you into the musical process. Considering the problem of making an organized noise with instruments will reveal to you the strategies underlying musical form, and eventually music's emotional, intellectual, and spiritual content.

We begin our exploration with a definition. We can define *orchestra* as any largish group of musicians and instruments gathered together to play music written for them. The actual size can vary enormously from, say, the seven people required to perform Bach's Brandenburg Concerto No. 6, to as many bodies as can be got together at one time. Even this initial observation about bringing people together to play music tells us something about the structure of the compositions intended for them.

As you may know, music in large forms, like a symphony or concerto, seldom plays continuously. It comes in chunks, called *movements.* There are pragmatic and artistic reasons for this. The artistic ones we'll deal with later. Pragmatically, as long as you've got all these people together expecting to be paid, you might as well give them something to do that takes longer than five minutes. In fact, it makes a great deal of sense to lump a series of smaller pieces together into a larger group; and by altering the volume, speed, and instruments in each piece, you can show off your orchestra to best effect.

This idea applies to virtually any music in which several people participate, and of course relates to our original point about music taking time, both to listen to and play. Remember also that several centuries back, concerts could last about five hours, and any five-hour concert consisting entirely of unrelated four- and five-minute snippets would have been pretty dire for the audience. But beyond these simple observations, a closer look at the history of the orchestra will tell us something about the kind of music that it was expected to perform.

If this were a music history text, we'd break music up into several periods: Renaissance, Baroque, Classical, Romantic, and Modern. Then perhaps a little chart would show what instruments were available to composers of the time, and you could see for yourself the fact that musical ensembles went from small to huge and back to small. Big deal, no? That is about all that music appreciation can do, aside from helping confirm your feeling that classical music has always bored and repelled you.

Instead of looking at charts of musical instruments, think about the orchestra on the basis of what you're going to hear. Consider two well-known pieces of music written for the same forces: Vivaldi's *The Four Seasons* and Mozart's *Eine kleine Nachtmusik* (A Little Night Music). Both use only strings—violins, violas, cellos, and basses. But wait a minute—if you listen closely to the Vivaldi, you'll hear a harpsichord or organ playing in the background. In fact, if you listen to anything written before about 1775 you'll hear a harpsichord or organ playing along. So here's a legitimate dividing point in the idea of orchestral sound. Call the time before 1775 "the continuo period," and the time after "the sonata period," and let's see what each type of orchestra tells us.

THE CONTINUO PERIOD

Instrumental music represents an exception rather than a rule. The vast majority of compositions, even by composers who became famous as masters of the orchestra, requires actual singing of one sort or another. In fact, the human voice was the first musical instrument, and it remains by far the most versatile and expressive. All other instruments embody some sort of modification of vocal technique: some are higher, lower, louder, softer, can hold notes longer, or can play several notes at once. But no single instrument communicates with the same directness and intensity as the human voice. This relationship between instruments and voices is the single most important fact about the orchestra. The differences in the treatment of instruments that we are about to discuss all stem from the various ways in which composers toyed with the vocal origins of musical instruments.

The orchestra is a fairly recent invention, dating back only about 350 years. Its origins lie in the groups of instruments gathered to play dance music at parties or festivals, and to provide accompaniments and interludes to the action of plays. The more instruments brought together, the bigger the noise, and the more accurately the music could describe the action of the spectacle. The principal purpose of the music was to *accompany,* be it dancing, speaking, or singing. The music was subordinate to some other activity, or to the meaning bestowed by the use of words. It was during the continuo, or Baroque, period (from around 1600 to 1775), that composers first tackled the problem of creating orchestral music that stood independently. Here's how they did it.

The first problem in assembling an orchestra lies in finding a group of instruments that sound well together. Stringed instruments fill the bill. They all belong to the same family; they have a decently wide range; they can play any note evenly; and they have a distinct advantage over the voice in that they can hold notes indefinitely since they do not require breath. Thus, violins, violas, cellos, and basses, along with their older relatives, the viols, became the foundation of the orchestra. The sound each produces corresponds to one of the four basic human voices in a chorus: soprano, alto, tenor, and bass. No other group of instruments would have fulfilled this basic requirement. Brass instruments didn't have valves, and so could not play evenly in different keys. They also did not blend well together. Woodwinds, such as flutes, oboes, and bassoons, sound thin and harsh in large doses, and they do not blend very well either. Clarinets hadn't yet been invented. Percussion instruments were good only for special effects, and were, in any case, limited to tuned drums (timpani) whose range included only a couple of notes, or to noisemaking devices of no definite pitch at all (such as cymbals, triangle, or tambourine).

Our first orchestra, then, consisted largely of strings. Any other instruments tended to act as soloists, set against the string background. But what about that harpsichord in the Vivaldi? Well, the purpose of the harpsichord was to accompany the orchestra by filling in the harmony, just as a piano or band accompanies a singer. Except in this case, the orchestra should be considered the singer.

One of the most interesting facts about the human voice is that whenever it appears with other instruments, our ears automatically try to focus on its sound and the expectation of words, thrusting everything else into a secondary position. If an orchestra, then, is to become the voice, then the Baroque composer needed to treat it as if it actually were one. And he knew that background, or accompanying, music made the voice's song more expressive. But there was still a problem. A group of instruments doesn't grab your ear as easily as a voice does. So the composer needed some instrument, or group of instruments, that would stay permanently in the background, and fill in whenever the orchestral voices soared off on their own. The harpsichord accomplished precisely this. The composer could also use an organ, lute, or guitar, and often had a couple of cellos or basses helping out with the bottom-most (bass) line to firm up the accompaniment. This "sub-music" was called the *con-tinuo,* because it provided "continuity" in the orchestral texture, linking the solo voices with the supporting harmony, yet never getting in the way of their singing. The continuo stood in exactly the same relation to the rest of the orchestra as the orchestra originally did to our singer, or play, or dance.

The fact that instrumental voices do not command attention like a human voice, far from being a disadvantage, created a host of new opportunities. If a composer sets a text, he generally wants the audience to understand what is being sung; therefore, he must restrict himself to one voice at a time, so the words remain clear. In the case of a chorus, they usually must all sing the same words simultaneously. But the orchestra has no such constraint. The composer need only convey a general feeling of the mood of the piece, and leave the specifics up to the listener's imagination. Rather than writing for only one voice at a time, he can use several at once, each one contributing to the general conception through its interaction with the others. And because there are no words, the ear has no trouble following the various musical lines as long as they balance and stand out against each other. This kind of writing for many voices is called *polyphony,* which, not too surprisingly, means "many voices." The practice of polyphony is called *counterpoint.*

In our string orchestra, the easiest way of bringing out additional voices would be to have one player, say, a violin, play solo. If we want more variety, we could add a trumpet, flute, or oboe—or even all three. The only limit to the number of voices is our ability to keep everything clearly audible. These solo voices stand in the same relationship to the orchestra as the orchestra does to the continuo. Whenever the solos play, the orchestra fades into the background. For this reason, Baroque orchestras tended to be small, lest the solos get swamped. In fact, many so-called orchestral passages often consisted of nothing but the solos and a few extra strings, all playing together (or *tutti*).

Let's try to imagine what music like this must sound like in terms of the basic elements of musical expression, which are tempo, dynamics, rhythm, melody, tonality, and timbre.

Tempo. This means the speed at which the music moves. Traditionally, movements take their names from tempo designations, which are usually in Italian.

Presto	very fast
Allegro	fast
Allegretto	sort of fast
Moderato	moderately fast
Andante	walking tempo
Lento	slowish
Adagio	slow
Largo	really slow
Grave (grahv)	one foot in it

As with everything musical, these terms are open to wide interpretation. One conductor's moderato can be another's allegretto. (The same indications often appear in German or French, depending on how nationalistic the composer wants to be, but Italian is the norm. Thus, you will often hear people refer to the second movement of Beethoven's Fifth as "the Andante.") And there are many qualifying adjectives that you can add to the basic tempo designation. But don't worry about these. You'll pick them up as you go along.

Now, what about our Baroque composition? Too much fast music will seem relentless, and exhaust the orchestra. Too much slow music is boring. We want to grab the listener's attention right away, so the beginning is usually lively or very loud and impressive. Some slow music in the middle will provide a nice contrast, and we can wrap up the whole operation with a zippy finale. But since we want to give the orchestra and soloists a good workout, let's make each tempo variation an independent movement, giving the work three major sections, fast-slow-fast.

Dynamics. To a certain degree, dynamics tend to be self-regulating in the Baroque orchestra. When the whole orchestra plays, it will naturally sound loud. The solos will be somewhat quieter, especially if we have to drop out part of the orchestra to hear them clearly. (Thus, detailed specification of dynamic levels was considered unnecessary until the Classical period, where it was regarded as a sensational innovation.) In any case, we have the continuo to accompany everyone and keep them together. (In those days, the conductor either played one of the solos or improvised the continuo part from the keyboard.)

Rhythm (or Meter). Virtually all rhythm boils down to units based on multiples of two (duple) or three (triple). Marches, for example, are almost always based on a rhythm of two (*one*—two, *one* —two), while dances often employ triple rhythms (*one*—two— three, *one*—two—three). Dance rhythms tend to sound more lilting and relaxing than march rhythms. But in any case, the choice of rhythm depends on the intensity of the music, and the contrast between the movements. One possible solution, for example, could be a quick first movement in duple meter, a slow movement, and then a more relaxed finale using triple meter. At slow tempos, the actual rhythm can be difficult to measure unless it is very clearly marked.

Melody. Quite simply, this refers to a good strong tune. Quick movements frequently begin with one but because there will be so much action in terms of motion and rhythm, the tune does not have to be unusually distinctive. In the slow movement, however, melody is everything. Here the soloist is given a chance to show off his expressive ability, just as the quick sections display his virtuosity.

Tonality. This determines what key (or note) functions as a sort of musical home base. We will talk about this extensively in the next chapter, but for now, all we need to understand is the fact that it makes sense to end in the same key as we began in, since doing so gives a feeling of unity to the composition. When our solo first enters, it might be a good idea to highlight the entrance by changing key, thus enhancing the independence of the musical material.

Timbre. This is the sound of the individual instruments. Each must be chosen so that together they sound well, and yet will stand out clearly during their solos.

* * *

So what have we got? Is all of this speculation merely the work of a feverish imagination? Let's look at "Spring" from Vivaldi's *The Four Seasons,* and see.

The first thing to note about "Spring" is that it's actually a violin concerto in three movements. *Concerto* simply means a piece for solo(s) with orchestra. The movements are arranged in a fast-slow-fast pattern—so I wasn't just making the whole thing up. Vivaldi marks the first movement Allegro (fast), and begins with a good, solid, bright, or "spring"-like tune. The tune consists of two phrases, each of which gets repeated, and the solo then enters with its first episode. Now it so happens that for these particular concertos Vivaldi wrote (or appropriated) four poems, each describing a particular season. The sections after the various statements and re-statements of the tune, called *episodes* or *interludes,* follow the stanzas of the poems. The first interlude describes the songs of birds, and two other soloists assist the principal violin in its avian imitations. After the birds, Vivaldi repeats a bit of the orchestral introduction *tutti* (meaning everyone plays it together).

Clearly, this movement will be organized on the principle of alternating tutti and solo sections. Altogether, Vivaldi gives us five solo sections representing, respectively: birds, a babbling brook, a storm (complete with thunder and lightning), more birds, and one episode left to the listener's imagination. These pictorial effects help make the form singularly clear. Between each section, some part of the opening tutti returns, and for this reason it is often called a *ritornello.* Finally, the ritornello concludes the movement after the last episode.

The second movement, Largo, moves so slowly that Vivaldi does not try to depict the range of incident captured in the first. This is a musical portrait of a country scene on a hot lazy day: the solo represents a sleeping shepherd; the monotonous violins sym-bolize the slight breeze rustling through the leaves of the trees; and the viola's loud "arf-arf" depicts the shepherd's trusty dog. Note that the entire piece consists of a long, meandering melody for the solo, balancing by contrast the almost kaleidoscopic variety of the first movement.

The last movement, another Allegro, does not return to the complexity of the first. The lilt of the music indicates a dance piece —a light triple meter, with which Vivaldi depicts a peasant celebration. Rather than marking very formal sections as in the first movement, the solo shares in the dance, leading it merrily along.

The fact that Vivaldi writes illustrative music in this case highlights rather than conflicts with the necessary contrasts within the musical structure of his concerto. You can forget about the poem entirely and still enjoy the piece. And remember that to the extent that instruments imitate voices, all music is illustrative. Vivaldi merely had something particular in mind here. The basic principles of opposition between solo and tutti passages are common to all works of this type. In continuo music for orchestra, a piece featuring a single soloist is called, not unreasonably, a *solo concerto,* while pieces for more than one solo fall loosely under the term *concerto grosso.* In a concerto grosso, any number of solo instruments alternate with the larger orchestra, though the ways of actually doing the alternating are infinite, as are the possible instrumental combinations. But admit it, it *was* easy to follow, wasn't it?

Now suppose we have an especially festive occasion, and we need something bigger than a concerto grosso. Maybe we have an unusually large (and expensive) orchestra, with trumpets and drums, and we want to get more mileage out of everyone. What can we do?

For starters, we can begin impressively with a grand and stately procession. This will grab the listener's attention even at a slow tempo, and especially if the rhythm is very strongly marked. Then we can show off our virtuoso band with a quick middle section in the flashiest contrapuntal style, rather like the solos in a concerto grosso. Finally, let's wrap the whole thing up in a fittingly imposing manner with a return of the processional. This gives us one big movement in three parts. This operation is called a *French overture.* If the pattern is closer to the concerto grosso—that is, fast-slow-fast, but not in separate movements—then the overture is *Italian,* and can also be called a *sinfonia* (sound familiar?).

Because the French overture itself tended to be rather overwhelming, and really too short for a grand festivity, it became customary to follow it up with a suite of popular dances, mixing different types based on duple and triple meters. Some of the options at the time were: *allemande, courante, gigue, sarabande, gavotte, minuet, badinerie,* and *hornpipe*—and you could use as many as you liked until you got a balanced assortment. For convenience, call the entire project an Overture.

Believe it or not, this is about all you need to know about the forms of Baroque orchestral music. These two categories, concerto (or concerto grosso) and overture (or sinfonia), cover just about every piece that Baroque composers wrote for their small orchestras. When the music has genuine solos, the form is exactly the same as that of a song (aria), with the instruments assuming the function of voices. Otherwise, the music either derives from stylized versions of marches and dance steps popular at the time, or demonstrates the composer's mastery of the contrapuntal style.

Now stop for a moment, and think about what we have discovered so far. All we have done is think about the challenge of inventing music without voices. In the process, we have discovered that the musical forms of those pioneering orchestral composers represent the simplest solution to the problem. Basically, they continued to write vocal music, but they took advantage of the instruments' wordlessness to enlarge the dimensions of their art. Of course, in writing this, *I* knew in which direction the argument was going, but the essential point remains: if you were a composer and found yourself confronted with the problems described in this chapter, and if you really thought about it, you would arrive at the same logical and unique solutions as Vivaldi, Bach, Handel, and their contemporaries.

The concerto grosso and the overture paved the way for an

entirely new type of musical art form. At the same time, the music of Vivaldi, Bach, and Handel is certainly mature and complete in itself. The history of music is not an evolutionary process from lower forms to higher ones. Rather, it depicts the endless struggle of composers with the same basic elements of musical expression: tempo, dynamics, rhythm, melody, tonality, and timbre. Any musical form based primarily on one of these elements involves some sort of trade-off in terms of the others, and each generation seizes on what it perceives to be an element left undeveloped by its predecessors.

Composers following the Baroque period asked different questions of their instruments. Taking for granted the idea that instruments were a legitimate substitute for voices, they wanted to know whether or not instruments could become self-sufficient. Did form have to depend on solos in opposition to a larger group? Must instrumental music be polyphonic? Was it always necessary to accompany all those instruments with the continuo? What element could free music from these dependencies? The answer: tonality.

4
▼

Understanding the Orchestra:
The Sonata Orchestra

THE ADVENT OF THE SO-CALLED SONATA
orchestra corresponds to the Classical period, the time of Haydn,
Mozart, and Beethoven. Their music, as you will hear for yourself,
sounds very different from the compositions of the Baroque period,
and it's organized along different lines. If we recall our list of the
primary elements of musical expression—tempo, dynamics,
rhythm, melody, tonality and timbre—we can say that Baroque
music was based primarily on melody, and the contrast between
tunes played by the full orchestra and those belonging to the solo.
When several solos participate, the contrast becomes even greater
owing to the difference between homophonic (tutti) and polyphonic
(solo) textures.

Sonata music, on the other hand, takes its form from the
tensions generated by changing tonality, or key. This is a much
more subtle and confusing subject than melody and counterpoint,
and it is complicated by the fact that most of what's taught by
music appreciation texts misses the point almost entirely. On the
other hand, the pieces written during the Classical period by its
three great composers include many of the most popular works in

existence, and are so convincing and appealing that they have given us the term "classical music." Surely music so universally acclaimed isn't organized according to some diabolically clever and obtuse scheme?

Naturally not; but tonality can be a tough subject to tackle because it's a quality unique to music. As we'll come to see, it's sort of like perspective in painting. Its characteristics are easy to define and understand, but also infinitely variable. Unlike the contrasts between solo and tutti episodes in Baroque music, changes of key frequently are not so much audible in themselves, but noticeable through the emphasis they place on other aspects of the composition, such as dynamics, melody, or timbre. The best way to understand tonality is to employ a threefold approach. First, we'll get familiar with the terminology. Next, we'll look at the effects of a change of key (or *modulation*) on musical form, with the help of an appropriate though somewhat offbeat analogy or two. Finally, we'll apply this knowledge in both this and the next chapter in order to understand the workings of the sonata orchestra and its music.

Like most things in our musical tradition, the concept of tonality evolved more or less randomly over the years. Different cultures have different tonal systems, but the function of a key, simply put, is to provide a recognizable musical location. In our system, there are twenty-four possible locations, each with its own name consisting of one of the first seven letters of the alphabet, with qualifiers:

C

C-sharp/D-flat

D

D-sharp/E-flat

E

F

F-sharp/G-flat

G

G-sharp/A-flat

A
A-sharp/B-flat
B . . . the next note is C again, etc.

The words "sharp" and "flat" are necessary because we have only seven letter names for twelve notes. For example, between C and D—a *whole step*—there is a note. "Sharp" means to go up to the very next note (the distance of a *half step),* in this case C-sharp. But you can also go "flat," or down a half step from a higher note, in this case D. So the note between C and D can also be called D-flat. It all depends on the direction you're coming from. And as you might have guessed, the fact that only seven letter names are used for twelve notes indicates that the sharps and flats, which correspond to the black keys on a piano, were later additions to our system. One of these, B-flat, happened along so close in time to the original seven, and was so often preferred to just plain B (or "B-natural" as it's called when it's not flat or sharp) that in Germany it actually acquired the letter B, while B natural is designated by the letter H.

"But wait!" I hear you cry. "We still only have twelve locations. What about the other twelve?" Well, each key comes in two varieties: *major* and *minor.* The differences between the two resemble the differences between vanilla and chocolate. Major keys tend to sound pleasant, stable, and run a certain danger of becoming bland if not used with enough contrast. "Happy" music generally sticks to the major keys. Minor keys, like chocolate, are richer, decadent, sinful, and may cause serious gastric discomfort, sadness and depression in excessive quantity. They represent instability, anxiety, despair, or just plain weirdness. No one is exactly sure why these emotional connotations hold true. They may stem from one last element of musical orthography.

Keys are arranged from their first, or home note, in a pattern called a *scale.* But although there are twelve notes, it takes only seven to make a complete scale, and this basic pattern of notes, each a fixed distance apart in terms of half steps and whole steps, always defines the major key. Minor keys, on the other hand, can use several different spellings, or patterns of seven notes, to make different scales. They must necessarily include "foreign" notes not part of the basic major scale. This in turn creates different relationships with all of the other keys. Perhaps for this reason, minor tonalities sound less secure and predictable. Once again, nobody actually thought this out. It just sort of evolved as composers attempted to impose order on the musical universe and thus harness its expressive potential.

Many factors go into deciding what key to use as "home." Sometimes, composers relate certain keys to specific emotional states. In our tradition, for instance, the key of E-flat major tends to be expressive of qualities of heroism, as in Beethoven's Eroica Symphony or Strauss's *Ein Heldenleben* ("A Hero's Life"). Also, instruments have different timbral qualities, depending on their method of construction, and some keys are more technically difficult on a particular instrument or may not sound as well. D major/minor, for example, seems a popular key for violin concertos, at least according to Beethoven, Brahms, Tchaikovsky, and Sibelius. But no matter what key we start in, the most important thing to listen for is where, and how far away, the music goes. The contrast is found in the distance between the different locations, rather than from any qualities inherent in the locations themselves. Let's look at how this might work theoretically, then practically.

Here you are, a budding Baroque composer writing a concerto grosso. You've chosen your tunes, and assembled a first movement all in one key, and you're bored but you're not sure why. The tunes are good ones, the contrasts clearly audible, but somehow it's just not very interesting. So you decide to work by analogy, and construct a model that illustrates the form of your new concerto. Because for you, as for all Baroque composers, the instruments represent actual voices, it's only natural to imagine your orchestra and soloists as a group of people gathered together—say at a party.

Like your concerto, it's a dull party. Perhaps it's late, and most of the food is gone. In fact, all that's left are a few drinks at one end of a long table, and a couple of cookies at the other. As you take a drink, you listen to the general buzz of conversation—to the orchestra in fact. Then, a couple of people come to get a drink, and the noise of the party fades as you focus on the conversation of these soloists. They take a drink, move off to get a cookie and leave you to the sounds of the party, then return for another drink, go for a couple more cookies, and move off. Here is your first movement, a simple series of alternating sections in which you keep hearing the same orchestral sound followed by snatches of the same conversation among the soloists. How can you devise a more interesting scenario?

Imagine that one of the soloists (the hungriest one) has called to have a pizza delivered, but to the back terrace so that the rest of the starving crowd doesn't find out. You follow the soloists outside, and in changing your location a remarkable thing happens. The topic of conversation changes, too. The soloists comment on the evening air, the pizza, the time of night. From your new spot even the sounds of the party assume a different character. Finally, the pizza makes everyone thirsty and you all return to the main room for a drink. You sigh with satisfaction as you realize that your problem has been solved. Changing key, or *modulating,* has given your concerto the interest it lacked. How? By forcing you to give your soloists a new theme to correspond to their new location, for one thing. Also, the music of the orchestra (the noise of the party), though clearly recognizable, sounded somehow different when heard from the perspective of the new key.

Now all of this imaginative theorizing is fine, but if it's to make any sense in the real world, there ought to be a way to hear what we have just described. So refer back to the first movement of "Spring" from Vivaldi's *The Four Seasons.* Because there is only a single featured soloist, Vivaldi heightens the interest by giving each solo occurrence an individual theme. But one section stands out above all the rest: the central episode representing a storm. The music moves suddenly into a minor key, suggesting anxiety. The solo writing must be more brilliant than ever to hold out against the raging orchestra, and when the orchestral ritornello arrives, it partakes of the same minor tonality.

Not only does a modulation to a new key make your music

more interesting, it enlarges the size of the movement as a whole. It took time to get to the terrace, eat the pizza, and rejoin the party. "Spring" exploits this tendency, but in a uniquely musical way that both supports our analogous situation but at the same time cautions against carrying things too far. The storm episode begins abruptly with no warning, as if our companions at the party had suddenly appeared on the terrace out of thin air, just like the comings and goings of the characters in "Bewitched." But having gotten into a dramatic new key, the music spends considerable time getting back out, since the minor-key version of the ritornello that follows the storm necessitates an entirely new solo episode solely for the purpose of getting home. Had the storm never occurred, it's entirely possible that the first movement of "Spring" would have been shorter by at least one section.

Despite the fact that Baroque music can and does change key, it tends to stay close to home. In other words, tonality is not the structural principle upon which the form is based. The contrasts that create the forms of continuo-based music are strong enough so as to require very little extra emphasis. If each entrance of a solo, or repetition of the ritornello, involved modulation to a distant key, not only would the movement be too long, it would break up into an incoherent series of detached episodes. Nevertheless, the idea of using tonality to organize music became increasingly appealing to early Classical composers as they explored the possibilities of the orchestra and its instruments.

Artists like to think of themselves as being original, innovative, and daring. Audiences like to be up on the latest styles and fashions. Sometime in the second half of the eighteenth century, composers began to feel that the language of Baroque music had lost its freshness. New instruments like the piano and the clarinet were being introduced. Orchestral music concerts (which always included vocal music, improvisations, and solo works) became public affairs, and the size of the orchestra grew to fit large halls.

At the same time, composers continued their exploration of things that instruments of the orchestra could do that voices could not. The endurance, range in pitch, and volume of the orchestra offered possibilities for greater contrasts and ever new sounds. In order to obtain these new sounds, the instruments had to begin to work together as never before, blending and supporting each other rather than standing out as solos. Instead of a group of many distinct, individual voices, speaking simultaneously and sometimes acting together as a single voice, composers employing this new, blended sonority began to think of the orchestra as a succession of themes, each of unprecedented range and power, which had to be presented sequentially, and which had the ability to interact dramatically. This different conception of orchestral sound produced both advantages and new problems.

The continuo orchestra operated on three distinct planes of sound: the solos in the foreground, the orchestra in the middle, and the continuo in the background. These three planes never mix, partly because of the way that the composer deployed his instruments, but more importantly because the form depended on maintaining the contrasts between them. In order to make the orchestra sound as one voice, these distinctions had to be eliminated. The obvious first step was to dump the continuo, thus forcing the orchestra to support itself, but the actual historical process was very gradual. Composers still assumed the presence of a harpsichord or piano, though probably because the composer at the piano could hold together an under-rehearsed orchestra and "vamp" in an emergency. The piano actually replaced the harpsichord as the continuo instrument of choice, because its dynamic abilities enabled it to better blend its tone with an orchestra in which the strict separation of foreground from background was no longer necessary.

In order to replace the continuo once and for all, composers had to enlist the aid of other instruments. Instead of standing out as solos, musicians had to work together to accompany whoever had the tune. Although strings remained the largest and most important part of the orchestra, flutes, oboes, clarinets, bassoons, horns, and trumpets began to appear regularly—not as solos, but in pairs that could blend and make harmony. The more instruments in the orchestra, the more interesting the composer could make his accompaniments, and the more richly he could color and inflect his tunes.

Even more importantly, the integration of the orchestra meant that the opposition of solo and tutti could no longer function structurally as the determinant of the form. This was because continuo-based structure often depended on the significant musical contrast between polyphonic (many voiced) and homophonic (single melody with accompaniment) textures. It was this alternation that made the distinction between solo and tutti clear in the small Baroque orchestra. Now, with so much of the orchestra busy with the harmony and accompaniment, there was only room for one tune at a time, maybe for the entire movement. Composers had to find a new organizing principle which would allow them to use their material creatively, without boring the audience to death.

Recall that any sort of musical form depends, as we have already noted, on repetition and variation. When we talked about changing key, we saw that it was an excellent way to enlarge the form, but because the contrasts in continuo music were already so strong, the effect had to be used sparingly. With these contrasts minimized, however, there is no reason for not using tonality as the major means of building a movement. Let's head back to our party and see what this form would look like.

Say that a friend has just called from the party to say that the crowd is great but the food is awful. So you intelligently decide to eat first, and then go. Our tonal structure begins at home. You spend some time eating, then you leave for the party, thus modulating (or traveling) from your home key or mood to a new location. While you're there, you meet people, go from room to room, maybe leave with a few friends and hit a few bars; in other words, you interact with other characters and this increase in action makes you change key more frequently. Finally, you're exhausted from an exciting night out and you head home for a good rest.

Here is a structure that uses tonality as its principal component. Notice the difference in focus between this sort of structure and that of continuo music. The subject of the concerto grosso was the *discussion* between the various soloists, interrupted and punctuated by the more imperious statements of the ritornello. But in this new form, *you* are the subject—your personality and experiences as you interact with other personalities defined by your travel through different keys. In sum, continuo music is argument, while our new form is drama and action.

An orchestral work written along with the lines of this new, dramatic framework gradually became known as a *symphony.* The general procedure is called *sonata form,* sonata simply meaning "to sound" in Italian. Like most musical forms, this one (and several of its variants) got codified into a textbook formula that very few compositions actually follow. But because you're likely to run into the official theory, we had better deal with it. This will at least help us to understand why such textbook formulations are more obfuscating than not and often a silly way to think about music.

A movement in sonata form (also called first-movement form) has three or four principal sections: *exposition, development, recapitulation, and coda.* The exposition begins with a first subject in the tonic (our home key), and then modulates to a second subject in the dominant (the one considered closest to home, actually five notes up from the tonic). This is then repeated. (We forget our wallet and have to go home for it.) The development section follows, running the material of the exposition through several keys, after which everything gets restated in the tonic in a recapitulation. Then the coda wraps the whole thing up. Clear? It's as dull to write as it is to read.

This so-called general view says nothing about why the form ought to be the way it is; and in fact, it's not even all that generalized. The kind of movement our textbook describes would look like the one we already mentioned, but with an additional character (the "second subject"—sounds like a psychology experiment): You're having dinner before going to the party. Meanwhile, in an apartment across town, an acquaintance is also getting ready to go. You both arrive at the party. Your eyes meet across the room. You exchange a few words, go out, hit a few bars, and wind up back at your place for some heavy interaction in the home key.

So you see, it's the same idea, only with more characters. What matters, actually, is not how many themes you have, but where you put them. You and your nine roommates could start out together. Your friend might bring someone else along. Forty-seven people might wind up having an orgy at your place, or at the party. It doesn't matter, as long as the locations (keys) provide enough variety for the themes, or groups of themes, to get repeated and varied creatively.

Now it should be clear why the textbook definition of sonata form is so useless. Just as no two people are alike, it is impossible to predict the number or personality of the characters in a sonata movement. Discovering this for yourself is one of the joys of listening. You may decide that each theme is a single individual, or that several themes in a given key define a personality. All you need to keep in mind is that each character sets out, has a series of adventures, and finally returns home changed by his or her experiences. The length, excitement, and emotional content of these adventures, their success or failure, depend on two people—the composer and you.

When the great composers of the Classical period—Haydn, Mozart, and Beethoven, but especially Haydn—invented this type of dramatic orchestral music, they weren't worried specifically about form as distinct from the other musical elements. Each piece was unique, and in any work of art, as we said at the beginning of this discussion, the form and content can't really be separated. The possibilities are endless, and composers invariably select musical materials with their goals in mind. For example, at the beginning of the twentieth century, Mahler and Nielsen discovered that you didn't always have to wind up at home at the end of a piece. You could spend the night at a friend's house, or even stay in a motel. This process came to be called "progressive" tonality, because the climax of the piece came upon attaining a goal that was in a different key from the one in which the piece began.

However many the possibilities, you can clearly see that any musical form tries to provide an audible framework for the series of repetitions and variations that allow composers to write instrumental music on a large scale. And if I seem repetitious *without* much variation, it is because this is an extremely important point. Everything in the next chapters stems from it. And just as the forms of music are as free as the composer's fancy dictates, so too does the composition and use of the orchestra vary from work to work.

It may seem surprising that in two entire chapters ostensibly about the orchestra, we don't really talk about the instruments, their history, and their individual characteristics in any detail. This is precisely the point. The best way to understand what the orchestra is *musically,* as opposed to historically or technically, is to discover what it does, and why. The ideas raised in simply thinking about the basic problems of writing for an orchestra lead us inevitably to its music. And as we have seen, the forms of orchestral music are not some very complex yet strict and rigidly imposed series of rules invented by genius theorists. Rather, they are the logical, practical, and above all imaginative solutions of the great composers to the basic problem of creating and organizing a language as rich, colorful, and emotionally powerful as the greatest poetry, without the use of words. Now it's time to learn that language.

5

▼

Forms and Patterns:
How Is Music Organized?

ALTHOUGH THINKING ABOUT THE ORCHES-
tra can tell us a great deal about its music, the fact remains that
each piece relates its own individual story. By now, you should have
a feeling for the fundamental ideas behind instrumental music. Our
analysis of Vivaldi's "Spring" gave you a chance to hear these principles at work in continuo music, and you should listen to the rest
of *The Four Seasons* yourself with an ear to the incredible freedom
and variety with which Vivaldi treats the concerto concept. Sonata
music created so much musical freedom of choice that we really
need to look at more than one example to see how such a revolu-
tionary language operates. In this chapter, we'll hear how four of
the great composers—Mozart, Haydn, Beethoven, and Brahms—
turned the theory of dramatic music into living sound.

At the beginning of our discussion of the orchestra, I mentioned Mozart's *Eine kleine Nachtmusik* as being written for virtually
the same combination (string orchestra) as Vivaldi's "Spring." Let's
take a closer look at the Mozart and compare.

Mozart: *Eine kleine Nachtmusik*

The full title of this wonderful little work is Serenade in G, K. 525, *Eine kleine Nachtmusik,* but fortunately we only have to know the more familiar later part. An orchestral serenade, which this is, is basically a lightweight symphony, often (though not in this case) with several extra movements that may incorporate a concerto and several dances. In this respect, it resembles the Baroque overture in its basic structure. But as you'll hear, there's nothing Baroque about the music.

First Movement: Allegro (Fast)

"Spring" began with a good, sturdy tune. Mozart starts off with a call to attention—an arresting fanfare designed to grab your ear. Only after this pronouncement does he throw out his first theme. The violins have it, and everyone else accompanies. But listen to how busy they are. The accompaniment doesn't just support the tune, it propels it forward, producing a feeling of motion and coiled energy.

Our textbook view of sonata form states that a movement like this should have three parts: exposition, development, and recapitulation. But that is not what really happens here. This first movement (and many other movements in sonata form) actually falls into two halves, the first half often being repeated, the second half less frequently so. The first half describes the journey away from the home key, while the second records the trials and tribulations of our character(s) as it (they) tries (try) to get back to the starting point.

After the brief introduction, the first half of the movement consists of a series of alternations between energetic assertions and quiet pleas for calm: a few samples of each mood, and the whole thing repeats itself from the beginning. This is the point at which you first notice that, in the process of presenting two different moods, you've actually gone somewhere.

The question of when to obey the composer's indication to make a large repeat is one of the most vexatious in all music. Some pieces benefit from the inclusion of the repeats, while others do not. In general, performers would do well to trust the composer with these matters. And even a literal repeat is much more than a mere dull repetition. As in the present example, most composers spend agonies trying to execute smooth transitions from one key to the next. This makes the repeat a new experience because up to that point we were unaware of how far we'd come. Also, the more you hear the main themes of the piece, the better you will be able to follow the adventures. And the net result of increased comprehension will be a feeling of the music being shorter and more concise— as opposed to when there are no repeats at all and you sit baffled, waiting for the music to stop.

The inclusion of the repeat in the present movement lets us know that, in spite of their charm and lightness, these tunes mean to *do* something. The second half of the movement begins with our opening fanfare—but it goes off in a different direction, only to be followed by the last tune we heard before the repeat. This little tune seems lost, wandering through a maze of keys until, seemingly ready to give up, the fanfare returns in its original form, and we're home. This second half might also be repeated, with the effect that our initial return home was too easily won, and required one more attempt.

So now you're probably saying to yourself, "Big deal! I didn't hear much drama." And if that's what you're feeling, then you're a good listener. This is a serenade, not a symphony, and the mood is lighter, more easygoing. The entire point of that little wandering melody is that, before it has a chance to get worked up about being lost, Mozart returns home and keeps the musical surface unruffled. But that means that the tension created between the vigorous tunes and the calm ones never quite resolves. And if the first movement can't decide what mood suits it best, maybe the issue will be settled in the second movement.

Second Movement: Romance (Andante—walking pace)

Nope. Not here. This is one of those svelte, sexy pieces that only Mozart could have written, and this kitten couldn't care less for any musical issues. She's content to purr, yawn, and occasionally stretch. Like the slow movement of "Spring" you should be as unconscious of form as the music itself seems to be.

Third Movement: Menuetto (Allegretto—fastish)

This is perhaps a bit more promising. The minuet is a little pompous, but definitely on the assertive side. It also has two halves, both repeated. But wait a minute: the middle section (or trio, as it's called) is very refined and elegant. Not a bit boisterous. And even though the return of the minuet (usually without the repeats) rounds things off, we still haven't settled anything. In fact, the two moods seem more opposed than ever, though perhaps the gracious way in which they take turns stating their case means that the opposition is at least friendly.

Fourth Movement: Rondo (Allegro)

Pay dirt! The elegant yet frisky tune that opens this movement combines the best of both worlds. A *rondo* is the sonata equivalent of the sort of circular structure that Vivaldi employs in the outer movements of "Spring." Statements of a ritornello theme alternate with episodes occurring in different keys. But, aside from reconciling the two moods presented in the first movement, this piece has its own business to mind. Notice how the episodes, those areas where the main theme displayed at the outset is *not* present, have a slight tendency to pull the music toward unhappier feelings (minor keys). It only happens for a moment, because before any seriousness sets in, our tune comes around again to put matters right. And in this mood of spirited gentility, the serenade draws to a close.

If you didn't hear any of the things that I'm talking about in this piece, don't be discouraged. In any instance where there are no words to clarify meaning, all I can do is try to convey my interpretation of what's going on. It's up to you to come up with your own impression if you can't agree with me. Chances are we'd both be right, since the inherent ambiguity in wordless music permits as many viewpoints as there are listeners. I may be the only person in the world who feels that the charm of *Eine kleine Nachtmusik* lies in its steadfast refusal to look at any of the potentially disturbing implications of its material. If you disagree, I challenge you to come up with your own scenario. Just be sure you can give yourself a satisfactory answer to two essential questions: Why is each movement a necessary component of the balanced structure of the piece, and, consequently, how do the movements work together better than they would separately?

Haydn: *Symphony No. 88*

Although the achievements of all great artists might be termed miraculous, Haydn is unique. In the years spent working for his patron in an isolated castle built on a Hungarian swamp, Haydn almost single-handedly invented instrumental music as we know it. His life was not tantalizingly tragic, like Mozart's, but Haydn's music bears eloquent testimony to one of the greatest victories ever of mind over matter. More important, although he spent much of his time writing opera and vocal music, Haydn was the first composer whose fame rests almost entirely on his instrumental music. He is the first great orchestral composer, and throughout his mature work he treats the instruments of the orchestra with a freedom and dramatic flair that have not dated one bit.

First Movement: Adagio (Slow)—Allegro

Haydn begins with a short, slow introduction—the Adagio. Like the beginning of *Eine kleine Nachtmusik,* the opening gesture serves to grab the attention. And yet, Haydn's real purpose remains obscure until we hear the actual first theme of the Allegro. The music is so quiet and simple that it would have been inconceivable to begin the symphony in this way.

Unlike Mozart, who delights in throwing off one ravishing melody after another, Haydn bases the entire first-movement Allegro on this innocuous tune and its accompaniment. Better yet, think of the opening of the Allegro as two themes presented almost simultaneously, one on top, the other on the bottom; first comes the top, then both together, at the first loud outburst. By presenting both characters at once, Haydn not only saves space (time), but has more freedom to play around. In fact, the clearly subservient position of the accompaniment has a dramatic purpose, as we shall see.

The first half of this movement, with the repeat, acquaints us with our two characters. The second half describes their travels, and no sooner does it begin than we find their roles reversed! The original tune becomes the accompaniment, and the accompaniment tries to overwhelm our timid tune. Notice how the conflict between the two starts to get more and more hysterical, the music veering toward minor keys until the orchestra breaks away wildly, pulls up suddenly—and we're home again, a little flute singing its relief along with the original tune. But no sooner do we think we're out of the woods than the accompaniment comes stomping in with a vengeance, and they're at it again. Realizing that quiet words are useless, the tune that started us off, along with the entire orchestra, shouts down the accompaniment and brings the movement to a close.

This movement demonstrates everything sonata music can do that continuo music could not. The whole span is based on one tune and its accompaniment. What's more, the independence of these orchestral voices from the continuo means that theme and accompaniment are reversible, an utter impossibility in the Baroque orchestra. The rapid movement through various keys produces dramatic conflict as our two characters wrestle with each other and the music attempts to restore order; and it's not until the very end that the conflict resolves itself through a dramatic change in the main theme's personality. The tune, so delicate as to need to be cushioned by an entire introduction becomes, through its experiences, assertive enough to conclude the movement in triumph. And all of this takes place in little more than seven minutes! The extreme compression and energy of this movement demands a contrasting relaxation, which we duly find in the second movement.

Second Movement: Largo

An oboe and solo cello together play a gorgeous tune in three quietly soaring arches, the sound of the two instruments evoking the Greek youth Narcissus tracing his reflection in a still pool of water. All is calm and indolent until suddenly the whole orchestra, with trumpets and drums, tries to shatter the idyll. If you're listening carefully, you may notice that the trumpets and drums were completely silent in the first movement. Haydn has saved them for this moment of surprise—a brilliant dramatic stroke. Fortunately, our self-absorbed youth proves utterly unruffled by this interruption, and, in spite of continued threats of violence, resolutely continues his meditation. That is the entire plan of this movement: a melody that the orchestra tries in vain to dislodge. Even in this supposedly relaxed interlude, Haydn finds room for some drama.

Third Movement: Menuetto (Allegretto)

This minuet is a rough, stamping dance with a quiet drum solo at the end of each phrase. The real prize, however, is the trio, one of the most picturesque and enchanting pieces of orchestration ever set down. You can use your own imagination in painting a mental picture of this music, but be sure to include bagpipes!

Fourth Movement: Finale (Allegro con spirito—with spirit)

Those violent interjections in the slow movement meant that in actuality it was the third movement that gave us a kind of respite from the dramatic conflict. The finale takes just about three and a half minutes to wrap up the entire issue in one great wave of musical comedy.

This movement, as with the Mozart, is a rondo with two episodes. Between each episode, the main theme recurs. The trick in listening lies in trying to guess when the tune will reappear. Only a full repetition of the theme counts, since Haydn tries to fool you by basing both episodes on the tune as well. The second episode is a canon (really a two-part round) in which the theme chases itself through the orchestra. Also, you may notice that the theme here bears a certain family resemblance to the allegro tune of the first movement. After a third and final repetition, the orchestra races away with so much energy that it takes three final chords to bring everything to a halt.

You should hear in this piece vastly more drama than in *Eine kleine Nachtmusik*. But when we speak of drama, tension, and conflict, keep in mind that the musical implications of these terms are not exactly the same as their theatrical ones. Haydn's Symphony No. 88 is one of his happiest works. The conflict in the first movement occurs within the context of overall high spirits, and the two characters fight like Laurel and Hardy as opposed to, say, the Allies and the Nazis. You must tailor your perceptions to suit the overall emotional range of the music. Haydn's is not only happy, but largely comic. The tension produced in sonata music reveals itself in the impression of constant movement and inexhaustible energy. Of course, music can represent the greater conflicts between good and evil, or hope and despair—and our next two examples do exactly that.

Beethoven: *Symphony No. 3 ("Eroica"—Heroic)*

Beethoven wanted to set the musical world on its ear with this symphony. By any standards, it's HUGE. This first movement alone is about as long as the entire *Eine kleine Nachtmusik* serenade, and the whole thing is more than twice as long as Haydn's 88th. But before we panic, let's think about this piece calmly, and above all musically.

If you wanted to write a quick movement almost twice as long as anything in music that had preceded it, what would you do? Remember our basic elements of musical expression, and consider that everything has to combine to make a very ambitious structure clear and comprehensible. The most important first consideration is melody. There are only two ways to write a big movement in sonata style based on various characteristic tunes. The first way is to write very long tunes. The second method, the one that we'll see in the first movement, is to write *lots* of tunes. And to delineate the structure of the piece, it would help even more to write tunes that are very different from each other.

I hope that you can see where this argument is heading without my also having to discuss rhythm, tempo, dynamics, and so on. The bottom line: in order to keep the audience's attention, a very long work has to be diverse, and all contrasts need to be emphasized. Paradoxically, the increase in internal complexity results in a compensating external simplification of form. Because the listener's long-range memory will be engaged for nearly an hour throughout this vast work, every major structural landmark has to be memorable. So although we may be dealing with more characters than ever before, and longer adventures, you may find the story easier to follow than you expect.

First Movement: Allegro con brio (Quickly, with verve)

No introductory messing around here: two sharp chords and we're off. Notice at once the extreme simplicity and memorability of the first tune, sung by the cellos. You may call this character our hero, if you like, and Beethoven has contrived that you will never fail to recognize him. One of the most impressive things about this piece (and you hear it immediately) is the fact that the orchestra sounds much larger than Haydn's, even though Beethoven added only one flute, one horn, and two clarinets to the ensemble. This means that the orchestra consists of strings, timpani, pairs of flutes, oboes, clarinets, bassoons, and trumpets, and three horns. Each tune gets its own unique instrumental color, and Beethoven treats the individual instruments with great freedom—except for the violins. Although they do a lot of accompanying and filling in, they hardly ever get to sing an entire tune. By throwing the weight of tone onto the lower strings, woodwinds, and brass, Beethoven achieves a darker yet harder sonority—a harsh almost militant sound that adds to the tense and heroic qualities of the music.

We saw with Haydn and Mozart that their first movements fell naturally into two parts. The first part led us away from home, while the second got us back. Beethoven follows the same basic outline, except that our hero spends so much time away, and has such a tough time getting back, that the movement actually falls into four parts. Part one, beginning with the cello tune already mentioned, we can call a portrait of Beethoven's hero, or the quality of heroism. Listen to the range of themes and the emotions they represent. Beethoven makes it easy to hear the end of this section: listen for six harsh, dissonant (clashing) chords, like someone banging a fist on a table, followed by a quiet bit of song and an emphatic stamping of feet that evaporates into wisps of the first theme.

The second part of the movement really sounds like an adventure. Beethoven introduces some new characters for our hero to meet, including a lovely song on the clarinets and oboes that just might represent a little love interest between battles. Listen carefully for the characteristic darkening of mood that heralds the arrival of minor (unhappy) keys, the tension created by the relentless repetition of anguished musical fragments, and the hero's unquenchable personality.

You should imagine for yourself the course of events in this second part. It takes up the bulk of the movement and is so full of incident that it doesn't seem as if the hero will ever get back home. The music begins to wander aimlessly, subsiding to a mere hush—a whisper of buzzing strings (called a *tremolo)* casts a fog over the orchestra. Suddenly, like a beacon, a horn spies a glimmer of light in the form of the first theme, and the whole scene brightens as the mists clear and the hero is back.

If you thought that this return seemed a bit miraculous, you were right. Although we hear all of the original tunes in their original order, the hero keeps wandering off, as though there might be something on his mind. No sooner do we reach the end of this third section, with the same pounding fist and stamping feet as earlier, than he runs away again. Perhaps he has a guilty conscience, for when the fourth and final part begins, we hear the lovely song that might be his beloved. Maybe it's my imagination, but whatever you call it, this tune represents the hero's final conquest, and a sweet one it proves to be. After a little interaction between the two characters, the orchestra blazes out with the hero's theme, and ends with the same two chords that started us off, plus one final slam in case you've missed the point.

The first movement of the Eroica Symphony is one of the most inexhaustible treasures of our musical civilization. Whether or not you think of it in terms of heroism, or as a series of fabulous tunes thrillingly orchestrated, the piece never appears identical on successive hearings. It demonstrates one of the great miracles of musical art: every emotion seems so clear and specific—but what is really being said? Listen to this movement carefully and consider the difficulty in describing something for which there are simply no adequate words. Try to get a feel for the emotional makeup of

Beethoven's hero. And forget about my imaginary labels for the themes—especially the one about the love interest. Then again, Beethoven was an excellent observer of human nature. And who ever heard of a hero who was sexually indifferent or, even worse, incompetent?

Second Movement: Funeral March (Adagio assai—"assai" means "very")

This movement represents the antithesis of the first. Just as Beethoven's portrait of our hero produced music of unprecedented power and nobility, the hero's death presents us with truly heart-rending grief. At the time of composition, this just might have been about the slowest piece of music ever written. Beethoven emphasizes the massiveness of the whole by making the first theme a march, but one broken-backed and dragging. Notice that the violins have the tune—their first real opportunity to sing. This is their moment—a lament sung out with a sort of suppressed melancholy that only stringed instruments can convey. If you're still uncertain as to the difference between major and minor keys, here is your big chance to get it straight. Think of our hero's tune in the first movement, and then listen to what has become of him here.

At the beginning of our discussion of this symphony, I mentioned that there are basically two ways in which to write very long movements: long tunes or lots of tunes. This movement gives us the long-tune method, which the extremely slow tempo only emphasizes. In form, the movement is a rondo, with two episodes and a coda. The first recollects happier things (major key), leading to a grand fanfare—a reminder of the hero's military conquests perhaps. The second episode is a *fugue,* a polyphonic (many-voiced) texture that reached its apotheosis during the continuo period. Basically, it's similar to a round (like "Row, Row, Row Your Boat"), written for any number of voices. An argument on a grand scale, the main theme of a fugue is appropriately called the *subject,* while any point at which the subject is not present is called an *episode.*

So much for technicalities. In this fugal section, the orchestra gets into a tremendous argument, each voice trying to surpass the other in eulogizing the hero. This reaches an extremely tense climax that is shattered by a menacing trumpet fanfare accompanied by tramping strings. Finally, the march returns decorated by woodwind palpitations, and in a long dying coda sinks back into darkness.

So far, in these first two movements, Beethoven has given us heroism, struggle, and a public sorrow of epic proportions. The emotions have been intense and unrelenting, but Beethoven has yet to finish his character sketch. In contrast to the seriousness of death, it's time to observe our hero at play. The formal elegance and restraint of the usual minuet would sound utterly out of place here. Instead, for the third movement, we get music as zippy as the second movement was draggy.

Third Movement: Scherzo (Allegro vivace—vivacious)

Like so much in music after Bach, the scherzo ("joke") was invented by Haydn, though Beethoven brought it to maturity as an instrumental form. Usually written in a triple dance rhythm, the scherzo can be, and often is, much faster, more capricious, and full of surprises. Its form is basically the same as that of a minuet: first part (usually repeated), middle section (still called a trio), and then the first part again (usually without repeats). The present example features whispering strings, chuckling woodwinds, and much hearty laughter. The trio is a *genuine* trio for once—three hunting horns accompanied by men on horseback gallop through a forest in pursuit of game.

Fourth Movement: Finale (Allegro molto—much)

Now we've got a problem. After all this activity, these tremendous swings of mood, what possible conclusion can there be?

How can Beethoven resolve all of the conflicting tensions thrust upon us by the previous three movements? Let's look at this finale closely, and see what he does.

First, the orchestra breaks out with a tremendous passage of preparation, only to be brought up short by disjointed *pizzicato* (plucked) strings. They play a sort of skeletal outline of a theme in two parts, each part repeated. We hear this entire process three times, each time with increasing animation from the rest of the orchestra. Suddenly, a new tune played by the oboes sails in, and we realize that the orchestra has gotten itself all worked up over nothing. The skeleton theme was nothing more than the bass, or accompaniment, to this delightful dance tune.

So far, in about two minutes of music, we have had two separate attempts to get started. There was the whirlwind introduction that led to a humorous anticlimax: the arrival of the skeleton-bass tune. Then, just as the orchestra was set to make do, in popped the oboe theme forcing the bass into its proper role as accompaniment. The orchestra takes up the dance tune, but seems to have second thoughts. Isn't this light, airy tune too trivial for what has gone before? The full orchestra gets into an argument over this question, and, as you might expect with a musical debate, proceeds with a fugue using the bass as the subject.

This first argument gets nowhere, and the tune tries to reassert itself, first in a very brilliant flute version, and then with a strenuous variation that sneakily tries to hide the theme beneath its serious exterior. Unfortunately, the orchestra isn't fooled. It picks up the argument (fugue) where it left off, culminating in a grand pause reminiscent of the whirlwind opening. But then what should turn up but the tune in a slow tempo, quietly and calmly pleading to be heard? And with the rest of the orchestra in full acquiescence, this little tune blazes out grandly one last time, crowned with trumpets and drums, thereby proving that it had the seeds of grandeur hidden within it all along.

Having thus demonstrated the tune's heroic aspect, the orchestra proceeds to congratulate itself in a satisfied sort of way, until suddenly the atmosphere becomes threatening. The orchestra trembles, reminiscent of the palpitations that accompanied the last appearance of the funeral march in the second movement. Suddenly the whirlwind introduction breaks out, vanquishing these premonitions of dread, and the brass section literally goes wild with joy as the symphony hammers its way to the final close. What can this movement be trying to tell us? Has Beethoven lost interest in his hero? He certainly says nothing more about him specifically.

In essence, the entire movement can be seen as an argument about whether or not that poor, common little dance tune has any right to be in the hero's company. Just as the orchestra seems dead set against it, the tune pleads for a hearing and shows its true heroic mettle. Maybe what Beethoven demonstrates with this tune is this: the symphony may be about a hero, but heroes are human, too. They live, die, and joke like the rest of us. And although you may just be an ordinary character, if you stand your ground and have faith in yourself, you have no reason to fear the company of the great. There is a little bit of the hero in all of us, and the important thing is not to let life intimidate you.

I can only add that as with Beethoven's view of his tune, so too with the music. Don't admire it from afar or feel intimidated. Participate, and make it a part of you.

Brahms: *Symphony No. 4*

Brahms chose as "home" for this work the key of E minor. Because minor keys tend to represent the unhappier side of life and because, contrary to popular belief, most composers were not morbid, maladjusted psychopaths, pieces that make minor keys their focal point tend to end happily. They do this by turning the minor key into the major, usually at the end, and after a great deal of orchestral hysteria.

The present symphony is one of the rare exceptions to the rule: a work that ends tragically. This does not mean that the piece is depressing. In fact, musical tragedy has precisely the same effect of catharsis that Greek tragedy purportedly produced on its audiences. The experience of mortality and the workings of an implacable fate against which we struggle in vain can produce a feeling of great exhilaration and, after having our emotions put through the wringer, at least a sort of satisfying exhaustion. Of course, the nicest thing about musical (and staged) tragedy is that it all happens to someone else, and we get a vicarious thrill out of suffering along with the victim, and all the while thanking the good Lord that it's not us.

First Movement: Allegro non troppo (not too)

This superbly organized movement falls into three big sections. The first, as we have come to expect, introduces our characters; there are four. First we hear a gorgeous, yet melancholy tune on the violins consisting of a chain of two-note sequences. This gets repeated and expanded by the woodwinds, until a jagged interruption leads to a second theme on the cellos, accompanied by pizzicato strings. It sounds an awful lot like a tango, and is far more passionate than the first theme. Next comes a happy dialogue between woodwinds and strings that leads to a sort of orchestral "cloud." Out of this emerges a noble, heroic tune—strongly rhythmic—on woodwinds and brass, first softly and then in full regalia. These, then, are our players. Listen to the way each one is contrasted in instrumentation, rhythm, and melody.

The second part of the movement throws these characters together in various ways—listen especially to the struggles of the heroic last theme. When its thrashings subside, you may catch the return of the first theme in a slow tempo, only to be obscured by the orchestral cloud we noted earlier. Suddenly, as though nothing has happened, we're home, and Brahms' happy idea of returning to the middle of the first theme suggests that the music is saying, "Why are you worrying? We were home all along!"

The return of the first theme initiates the third and final section of the movement, in which all of the themes appear in order. The heroic theme doesn't bring this section to a close, as it did the first but resumes its strenuous striving, as in the second. So just when you think that victory has finally been won, the mood darkens and the serene first theme appears, now vicious, in the full orchestra, its two-note phrases whipping through the instruments in lacerating fashion. This is the fulfillment of its tragic destiny. Having thus reached the utmost violence, the movement draws to a stormy close. There are no literal repeats at all in this movement. The action proceeds in one great sweep, tragic irony implicit in the fact that the most rhythmically regular, elegant, and emotionally ambivalent theme in the entire movement should be the agent of catastrophe.

Second Movement: Andante moderato

The first theme has a legendary, solemn character that sounds at once consoling and somehow mysterious. Its regular phrases and repeated hovering about one note give it the quality of ritual speech, like poetry or prayer. I leave it up to you to determine the actual story being told. Perhaps it concerns the second theme, a warmly romantic song for strings that appears like a vision of some lost beauty? Or maybe it recalls some recent conflict, such as that evoked by the tempestuous passage for full orchestra at the movement's climax. But while the music presents much that is alternately beautiful and terrifying, it feels somehow unreal, an impression heightened by the way it finally vanishes into an orchestral mist.

Third Movement: Allegro giocoso (jolly)

Here we have a furious attempt to attain happiness, assisted by a manic triangle that tries to propel itself into a state of euphoria.

The opening minute presents three independent themes, each short, jubilant, and rhythmically distinct. (A more lyrical fourth theme eventually follows.) This outpouring of joy relieves some of the tension that the first movement generated, and that the second movement seemed to avoid, but the whole thing is too forced, too frenzied—and, most important, too short. It's all over in about six minutes, leaving the listener with a feeling of having been trampled by an entire New Orleans Mardi Gras parade.

Fourth Movement: Allegro energico e passionato

The first movement gave us a tragedy. The next two movements represented two reactions to that experience: an escapist fantasy, and a desperate attempt to be happy in spite of it all. The fourth movement refuses to put up with this illusion. Far from explaining the tragedy, or resolving it, this movement simply confronts us with a reality from which no escape is possible. Brahms explores the entire range of tragic emotion from rage to solemnity, pathos, and resignation.

The form of this movement is one of the most ancient in music. It's called a *passacaglia* (pronounced with a silent *g*). Remember the bass from the finale of Beethoven's Third? Well, a passacaglia is simply a bass line that repeats itself over and over throughout the entire movement, and over which the composer can do just about anything. In this case, the bass consists of eight notes announced at the opening of the movement by the trombones and horns. And thereby hangs a tale. (Yes, another one!)

Up until the last movement, the orchestra of this symphony was virtually identical to that of the "Eroica," with the exception of one additional horn in the first two movements, and a piccolo, triangle, and contrabassoon in the third. Even so, this music sounds much bigger and above all thicker than Beethoven's. There are several reasons for this, but the principal one stems from the fact that Brahms employed a much larger string section than Beethoven, so his writing for those instruments is much richer and more luxurious. But this also makes it difficult for single wind instruments to stand out against such a strong background. Hence the need in loud passages to pit entire sections of the orchestra against each other, often with the brass instruments functioning more on a rhythmic than melodic level.

Brahms' last movement, however, brings the brass section of the orchestra to the fore with the addition of three trombones. In Western musical tradition, the solemn tone of trombones has long been associated with religious ritual, or with the supernatural. For example, in Mozart's opera *Don Giovanni* the title character literally gets sent to hell by a living statue to the sound of trombones. In German, the words for the last trump foretelling Judgment Day really translate as "the last trombone." Thus, in giving his passacaglia theme to the trombones, Brahms uses the instruments according to their most original function, though the truly weird harmonies they play are his own modern touch. (Now you certainly don't need to know this bit of trivia to understand the piece, but it's interesting all the same.)

On top of the passacaglia theme, Brahms evolves a series of meditations on the nature of tragedy. This is intense, emotional music, but it is *not* dramatic. It's certainly monumental, but, keep in mind, monuments don't usually travel. Perhaps if you call the passacaglia theme a representation of the omnipotence of fate, then you'll have some idea of what's going on. You may not always hear the bass, but it's there in the background, waiting, crushing hope, resisting all efforts to evade it. Of course, this is precisely what the orchestra tries to do, and its fruitless efforts only serve to increase the feelings of rage with which the symphony ends.

We've now listened to four pieces, all in four movements, all supposedly in sonata form. But as you can see, they don't have a great deal in common on close examination. Mozart wrote an elegant entertainment, Haydn explored the range of musical humor, Beethoven taught us the meaning of heroism, and Brahms gave us tragedy. Even the same instruments were made to sound different in the hands of these four composers. Yet we can derive a few general ideas from what we have heard:

1. Sonata music is essentially dramatic. What matters is not how many themes we have, or how long they are, but what happens to them in the course of the movement. This is in turn determined by tonality, though we only perceive tonality in terms of the dramatic interaction of themes. So form and content, as I've always insisted, are virtually indistinguishable, and I've probably gotten myself into enough trouble trying to take these four pieces apart.

2. Always listen for the way in which the individual movements cohere and create an emotional balance. When each succeeding movement sounds inevitable, then you are beginning to understand the long-term musical argument. If you think the piece would be better off without the slow movement, then you are not listening attentively. But also remember to give yourself time and several hearings. It took me years to get through the "Eroica" funeral march, even though its form is very simple and its emotional meaning rather clear.

3. Listen without preconceptions. Let the composer tell you his story, and try to meet him on his own terms. Because the forms of sonata music are so free and adaptable, they can encompass Baroque styles such as fugue, canon, and passacaglia, and use them in a manner consistent with their original meaning as part of a larger dramatic framework. In other words, you will never know what to expect, and this should not be disconcerting. I mean, who goes to see a horror movie or a comedy knowing in advance what's going to happen?

It's entirely possible that, having run out and purchased the pieces discussed in this chapter, you are feeling that I've made this whole thing up and you want to brain me with my own book. If this is the case, before you get violent, try reading the next chapter and then come back to this one. I think that you'll be pleasantly surprised at your progress. On the other hand, I made sure that my picture is nowhere to be found in this book—just in case I'm mistaken, and you decide to come after me.

6

▼

Musical Memory:
Training the Ear to Recognize Musical Ideas

IN THE PREVIOUS CHAPTERS, YOU MAY HAVE
noticed that all of the pieces discussed required one essential quality for comprehension: memory. Without a good memory, you will
not hear the return of various themes. Even more important, you
will not recognize those themes after they have changed or evolved
as a result of their encounters within a movement. Understanding
any music without words presupposes a solid musical memory, but
this is something that can hardly be taken for granted nowadays,
when our attention span is rarely taxed for more than five minutes
at a time. Fortunately, composers long ago came up with a musical
solution to this problem—the *theme and variations*.

A theme and variations is a piece of music in which the composer either writes or borrows a tune, and then manipulates it—for
example, plays it backward, changes its key from major to minor,
or adds an interlude or two between notes or phrases of the original
tune. Originally, it was an improvisational form. A composer
would give a concert and then as a finale challenge the public to
come up with a tune in order for him to impress them with his skill
at impromptu composing. (This particular concept of the theme

and variations still lives in the performing styles of many of our best jazz musicians.) However, the form soon took on a life of its own as composers set down their variations on paper. Listening to these pieces makes an ideal way for you to train your own musical memory, since they consist of systematic explorations of one single theme or idea.

As noted above, there are literally zillions of ways of varying a theme. You can play with the melody, adding or subtracting notes, make it longer or shorter, change the rhythm, speed it up, slow it down, just use a little bit of it, or play it upside down or backward. Or you can ignore the melody entirely, and concentrate on its harmonies, building entirely new tunes on top of them. Or you can follow the rhythm of the theme but with different notes, or play with the bass, as Beethoven did in the last movement of the "Eroica." And, of course, you can combine all of these techniques at will.

In many of the examples that we'll discuss, it's impossible to detect the actual theme in the variations, though its presence is in the background. When this happens, try to get a feel for a correspondence that you can't hear specifically. There are entire families of themes that share certain characteristics independent of melody. Identifying tunes based on the same musical elements is not only great fun, it illuminates the very nature of musical language by establishing connections between ideas that may, at first, seem unrelated.

The works discussed in this chapter do not require extensive analysis. I will try to clue you in on what to listen for; you take it from there. The most important rule in listening to music of this type is to *know the theme*. If you must, play it several times. Get it into your head. Hum or whistle it to yourself if you can. Composers almost always pick themes that give them room for development, so they tend to be catchy and easily recognized. And, as with any music, be sensitive to the emotional range of each work. Musicians find the most amazing feelings in the unlikeliest places. Ready? Here we go.

Ravel: *Boléro*

This is the simplest form of variation, since nothing about the theme changes except the orchestration. Ravel simply intended to create a huge orchestral crescendo *(crescendo* means gradually getting louder; its opposite is *diminuendo),* using a vaguely exotic tune propelled by a monotonous snare drum rhythm. Listen carefully, first to the theme, and then to the instruments as they play it, one by one. The theme falls into two halves, each half repeated—until the final time through, when the whole orchestra plays the tune just once. (Incidentally, this AABB structure will characterize many themes used for variations.) Even in this study of repetition, Ravel subtly heightens the tension before the great climax, in which you actually *hear* the music change key.

Liszt: *Totentanz* (Death Dance)

The title may sound gruesome, but the piece is actually a lot of fun. The theme, announced right at the beginning, is one of the oldest and most impressive of Gregorian chants: the *Dies irae* (Day of Wrath). The text of this particular chant comes from the Requiem, the Catholic Mass for the Dead, and describes the horrors of Judgment Day. It is one of the most widely quoted tunes in Western civilization. (If you saw Kubrick's film *The Shining* you might recognize it here.)

Liszt, one of the greatest pianists of all time, wrote this piece for piano and orchestra. The advantage in having a solo instrument is that the solo can do all sorts of flashy stuff with the theme, while the orchestra keeps our memories active with the original. That is more or less what happens here. However, since the theme's so short, Liszt breaks up the variations with brilliant passages for the soloist alone (called *cadenzas).* The *Dies irae* is a very easy tune to get into your head; you'll enjoy the gloom and doom, B-movie horror-flick treatment that Liszt gives it.

Rachmaninoff: *Rhapsody on a Theme by Paganini*

Like the Liszt, this too is a theme and variations for piano and orchestra, though the variations are far more strict. Everything relates to the theme, which does *not* appear immediately. Rachmaninoff ingeniously begins with the first variation as an introduction, and follows this immediately with the actual theme, announced by the violins and outlined by individual notes on the piano. As in *Boléro,* the theme comes in two halves, both repeated. Only here, the second half usually gets varied on repetition. After the strings announce the theme, the piano takes it up, and then anything goes. But you may notice the *Dies irae* putting in an appearance. Rachmanioff was obsessed by this tune. It appears in virtually everything he wrote, and in this particular work four times: three times toward the beginning (the first two times in the piano), and once at the end in the full orchestra.

In listening to this piece, the first half of the theme is by far the most important. It is almost always present somewhere in the orchestra, while the piano rhapsodizes on its emotional implications. Notice how the variations tend to group themselves into large units of similar character. The climax of the work occurs at the eighteenth variation: one of the all-time great knockout tunes ever written, based on the theme played upside down! Don't try to count the variations in anticipation. You can't miss this one. Finally, after the last appearance of the *Dies irae,* the very end is one of the funniest moments in music, a fabulous exercise in the art of anticlimax.

Britten: *Variations and Fugue on a Theme of Purcell*

This work is also known as The Young Person's Guide to the Orchestra, and if you want to know what the individual instruments of the orchestra sound like, this is the piece for you. Many composers choose a favorite tune of a famous colleague as the subject for variations, and this is a typical example. What better way to pay a musical compliment? Britten begins with the theme announced by the full orchestra. The theme is in a minor key, but then the woodwinds play a major-key version of it, followed by the brass, strings (including harp), percussion, and the full orchestra again in its original form and key. So actually you get five variants of the tune before the variations formally begin. Each instrument gets a variation to itself, from highest to lowest within each instrumental family: piccolo and flutes, oboes, clarinets, bassoons; violins, violas, cellos, basses (pitted against the woodwinds), harp, horns, trumpets (with snare drum), trombones, and tuba; and finally the percussion, including timpani (kettledrums), whip, gong, cymbals, xylophone, triangle, and so on. Britten then reassembles the orchestra in a fugue, each instrument entering in the same order as in the variations from flutes to percussion. The subject of the fugue is new, and once the percussion have slammed it about, the brass make a triumphant entry with the major-key version of the Purcell tune while everyone else continues the fugue, and so on to the rousing conclusion.

This piece is a classic case of variations where you may or may not detect the theme. Nevertheless, if you take note of each of its phrases separately, you will be able to figure out the variations eventually. The two most recognizable phrases of the theme, common to most of the variations, are the three ascending notes at the beginning and the little seven-note melodic turn at the end of the first phrase. Keep these in mind while you enjoy each variation in its own right for the witty and brilliant characterization that it represents.

By the way, this piece is available with narrative. *Do not* buy this version. You will want to listen to it as music, not as a school lesson.

Dvořák: *Symphonic Variations*

The tune on which Dvořák bases his variations is his own invention. It has three parts: a haunting, very Slavic folksong-like phrase, a rising sequence, and a repeat of the first phrase. Because the theme is so short (it takes only about thirty seconds to play, even at a slow tempo), the variations tend to fall into groups similar in mood and resembling the movements of a symphony—hence the title. Remember that first phrase, and you'll never be lost. This set of variations also culminates in a fugue, based on the by now familiar first phrase. In our original concert situation, improvising a fugue would have been (as you can well imagine) the height of virtuosity. In this case, a fugal finale makes a grand and imposing climax to a form which by definition tends to sound sectional. There's nothing like an argument to tie everything together at the end.

Brahms: *Variations on a Theme by Haydn*

The theme here follows the traditional format: two halves, both repeated. Although longer than the Dvořák theme, its shape is amazingly similar—an opening phrase, a rising sequence, and a return of the opening phrase. Brahms doesn't choose to stick to the melody of his theme all that closely. Rather, he follows its basic harmonies. This means that he can write very free-sounding variations. There are only eight of them, many with varied repeats, and each one a little character sketch rooted in the theme. So don't worry about hearing the original melody. Rather, get a sense of each variation's overall shape—the way it rises and falls, the ebb and flow of tension in its middle, rising phrase. As in his Fourth

Symphony, Brahms' finale to this work is a passacaglia (a series of brief variations over a recurring bass line), based on the first phrase of the theme.

Elgar: *Enigma Variations*

This splendid work represents in many ways a logical culmination of the theme and variation concept. The variations—each a complete transformation of the initial, lengthy theme—represent the composer's friends. Elgar has realized to delightful effect the tendency of the self-supporting orchestra to color a tune so as to give it personality and emotional depth—in a word, to *characterize.* The tune has a basic shape similar to Dvořák's, but like Brahms', it is much longer. The opening phrase of the theme is the one easiest to spot in most of the variations, and the first four notes can be sung to the composer's name: Edward Elgar. The prize variation of the lot is "Nimrod," one of the great symphonic slow movements packed into a very small space. The final variation is a self-portrait of the composer, sometimes heroic, sometimes introspective, but always brilliantly alive. Listen not only to the theme, but to the orchestration, for this is one of the orchestral repertoire's great showpieces. Try to identify the emotional character of each variation before checking the record notes to see whom it actually represents.

Walton: *Variations on a Theme by Hindemith*

Walton's theme is actually a large section of the slow movement from Hindemith's Cello Concerto (1940). It sounds almost like a lullaby, with a poignant second phrase that Hindemith had used earlier to represent the birth of the Virgin Mary in his song cycle *The Life of Mary.* This tender phrase leads to a wandering passage in dialogue between strings and winds. Eventually the entire first section returns, followed by a peaceful close that slowly dies away. In essence, then, the theme has four parts, the first and third being identical. That poignant second phrase is the one to remember in listening to the nine variations. According to Walton's scheme, the odd variations slow down, while the even ones speed up. The finale, after a series of great orchestral flourishes capped by cymbal and tambourine rolls, is really a series of fugue-like passages, each one based on a separate phrase of the theme. These build up until the whole orchestra dances with energy. A chime sends the dancers reeling home, and the theme returns, more serene and beautiful than ever. The final chord features each section of the orchestra in turn—a lovely effect.

Dutilleux: *Metaboles*

Dutilleux is one of the greatest living French composers. His *Metaboles* is a wonderful display of gradual metamorphosis: five sets of variations in which the initial idea—whether melodic, rhythmic, harmonic, or simply timbral—changes until it becomes the subject of the next set. The five linked groups have titles: "Incantatory," "Linear," "Obsessive," "Torpid," and "Flamboyant." The first group is sort of a *rondo* (see our discussion of *Eine kleine Nachtmusik* in Chapter 5) based on texture more than tune; the second is for strings only in long supple melodic curves. The "Obsessive" variations are a strict passacaglia—a very clever characterization as we know from our previous discussions (in the last chapter and here, both in connection with Brahms) of this repetitive form. The fourth group is a series of static chords that don't seem to want to go anywhere, but which finally give way to a flashy scherzo in which you may catch the return of the opening at the very end. This is a terrific, challenging piece that is difficult to grasp after only one hearing. It lacks themes that stay easily in the mind. But if you're feeling a little adventurous, then this one's for you. It rewards repeated listening like few pieces you'll ever hear.

* * *

When listening to these works, I suggest that you come to grips with each one individually, and then move on to the next. Take them in any order you want, though I have tried to arrange them in order of increasing difficulty. Remember that what is important is to keep listening. After hearing any of these pieces a few times, go back and listen to one of the works in the previous chapter. I think that you'll be amazed at how much more you will be able to pick up. All music is repetition and variation. If you can train your memory to recognize musical ideas, then you will have all the tools you need to find pleasure, and adventure in listening.

7

Large Forms in Small Packages:
Chamber Music

PERHAPS NO SINGLE CORNER OF THE CLAS-sical repertoire has inspired so much snobbery, mystification, and just plain nonsense as what has become known as *chamber music*. The very term, which implies something small, usually appears hand in hand with aficionados' claims to having experienced pure sublimity past the point of mortal understanding (or were they bored to tears but are afraid to admit it?). What's really going on here? We certainly have more than the usual number of myths to dispel in considering chamber music, but the effort builds so easily on what we've learned so far that by the time we're through, you'll surely be wondering what all the fuss was about.

The very concept of "chamber" music has meant different things at different times in our musical history. With music from the continuo period, the small size of the Baroque orchestra makes the distinction between chamber and orchestral music especially difficult to pinpoint. It could be argued that the number of instruments matters less than the type of music being played. A concerto, as we have seen, is generally considered to be an orchestral form featuring a soloist, or group of soloists, accompanied by the larger orchestra. But then we run up against Bach's Italian Concerto for harpsichord solo, which certainly embodies the concerto principle even though its single instrumentalist qualifies it as chamber music.

In fact, Baroque instrumental music that is not explicitly orchestral does have a category of its own: the sonata. Obviously, this term means something very different in the continuo period than it does for later composers. The ritornello or aria-based structure typical of the Baroque concerto remains the same in any sort of instrumental music requiring the presence of the continuo. A solo sonata, say for flute or violin, will usually require two or three players: the soloist and the one or two who comprise the accompaniment—usually a harpsichord and a cello (the cello is sometimes dispensed with). The most popular Baroque type of chamber music was the so-called "trio sonata," meaning a work written for three solo parts in addition to the continuo, for a total of four or five players. Already we're very close to Bach's sixth Brandenburg Concerto, which requires a mere seven players and which is considered orchestral.

To put these concepts into perspective, let's look briefly at a collection of trio sonatas, those for two oboes and bassoon by Jan Dismas Zelenka. Start off with the Sonata No. 5 in F major. (There are six, and you'll probably have to buy the whole set. Don't worry, it's worth it.) This piece is in three movements, like many Baroque concertos, and follows the customary fast-slow-fast pattern. In fact, both the first and last movements follow the same alternating pattern of ritornello and solo that we saw in Vivaldi's *The Four Seasons*. The other five sonatas are somewhat different, however. They have four movements each, arranged slow-fast-slow-fast, a form generally known as a "church sonata" because of its use of the polyphonic style in quick movements, and its descent from devotional music used during Mass. (Another type of Baroque sonata, the "chamber sonata," incorporates dance movements, and is not used by Zelenka in this series of works.)

The difference between orchestral and chamber music in the continuo period is thus, at least as far as terminology goes, a technical matter imposed from a later historical perspective, rather than anything inherent in the actual writing for the instruments. In fact, the whole matter is neatly summed up by Georg Philipp Telemann in his delightful set entitled *Tafelmusik* (Banquet Music). Arranged in three "productions," each part begins with an orchestral overture and suite, followed by a quartet, a concerto, a trio, a solo, and an orchestral conclusion, all of course with continuo. Since these pieces were presumably meant to be played in a dining room—however large, a dining room is no concert hall—we can assume that for most Baroque composers the distinction between orchestral and chamber music was a question of little significance, and leave it at that.

In the Classical period things become a bit more complicated. When we looked at the orchestra of the sonata period, we noticed that the main achievement of classical composers was the creation of a dramatic orchestral music based on tonality. This required new ways of writing for instruments, and a consequent abandoning of the continuo (though the habit persisted for practical reasons well past the point of its being musically necessary). One man, Haydn, was largely responsible for this new technique of composition, and the medium in which he first realized it to the full was one of his own invention: the string quartet.

It would be wonderful to be able to say that Haydn dreamed up the string quartet because he immediately realized its potential as the vehicle for the most profound thoughts in Western music. But in reality, it seems as though he found himself writing for an extra violin instead of the usual three players (string trios for violin, viola and bass being rather more common at the time, owing to the hardiness of the trio sonata concept), and simply adapted himself to local circumstances. In fact, controversy still rages about whether or not the bass instrument with the two violins and viola was intended to be the cello rather than a double bass. The reason that people should care about this we'll come to in a moment.

These early quartets (there are ten of them) are loosely structured, highly entertaining five-movement affairs, and they were a smash success throughout Europe. Naturally, the composer wanted to capitalize on their popularity, but because the public wanted novelty, and because as a musical genius he realized he had something extraordinary on his hands, Haydn did more than merely repeat himself. The old-style string trio, for either two violins, or violin and viola, with an unidentified bass, is really a trio sonata for two melody instruments, with the third part built into the accompaniment. As with any continuo music, melody and accompaniment remain fixed. What Haydn discovered was that use of a cello as the bass instrument, without harpsichord or additional help at harmonic "filling-in," created an ensemble of melody instruments, all potentially soloists. Anyone could take the melody or the accompaniment, and the four players of a string quartet were thus free to develop their own unique personalities and participate in a new type of dramatic dialogue. This explains the reason for the controversy about Haydn's bass. At what point did this revelation actually hit him? A useful question for historians perhaps, but it shouldn't vex us any further.

The string quartet rendered the continuo unnecessary, because any three instruments can comfortably form a full mass of supporting harmony. But this also required a new type of formal organization. Why? For the same reasons that applied to orchestral music. Baroque ritornello forms assume the presence of the continuo: everyone plays the tune together in the tutti sections, and the instruments take off on their own during the solos. This is clearly impossible in a situation where the same instruments playing the melodies are also responsible for providing their own accompaniments. In his Six Quartets, Op. 20 (nicknamed the "Sun" Quartets), Haydn accepted tonality as his new basis for musical organization, and the classical sonata style was born. The term *chamber music* has a specific meaning within this new style: music for a set number of players, which is sufficient unto itself and requires no additional support.

The subsequent history of chamber music can be seen as an evolutionary process in which different instruments are combined and coaxed to work together on an equal footing—without any giving up its self-sufficiency. The invention of the piano, which unlike the harpsichord has the ability to play softly and sustain notes over long periods, radically influenced this process. With its introduction weaker instruments could now participate without being overwhelmed, and without the piano part itself seeming inhibited. Each instrument in the chamber ensemble has both an independent and a collective role. This dual aspect of the participating instruments gives chamber music that characteristic sense of interaction and unfolding so typical of dramatic, tonally organized compositions.

None of this should sound all that complicated after the issues discussed in previous chapters. In fact, chamber music is in many ways easier to follow than orchestral music. Consider the advantages and disadvantages in light of our basic elements of musical expression:

Tempo. There's not much difference between chamber and orchestral music, other than the fact that fewer people are easier to keep together. It therefore follows that sudden changes of speed or greater extremes are possible in chamber music, but in practice this isn't all that significant.

Dynamics. Here orchestral music seems to have an advantage. An orchestra can play just as softly as and far more loudly than a string quartet. But remember, a string quartet was designed for a small room, and anyone who has lived next to a string player knows just how loud they can sound. After all, in most violin concertos the soloist manages to keep the entire orchestra at bay. In the proper setting, dynamic excitement doesn't have to be seriously compromised, though direct comparison naturally favors the orchestra.

Rhythm. Again, as with tempo, having fewer players may mean a gain in rhythmic accuracy, but it does entail a loss in terms of impact and emphasis.

Melody. In chamber music, everyone gets to play the tune, but, as with orchestral music, not every tune sounds equally well on all instruments. This of course is the one advantage of a homogeneous ensemble like a string quartet. What one can play, they all can play. Any other combination inevitably provides the composer with a greater challenge.

Tonality. This is a quality that functions utterly independent of the means employed in creating it. A strange modulation to a distant key is equally startling no matter who's playing, and matters of emphasis really belong under "dynamics." In other words, you may notice the modulation more if it's played by a twenty-piece brass section, but structurally the effect (which is to enlarge the form) will be the same.

Timbre. Here is the one area in which the orchestra has a plain advantage. It can produce a greater variety of sound, and some of these sounds can function to define the form (for example, a tune that is always played by an oboe may appear at crucial points in the musical drama). But this means that chamber music must compensate by emphasizing something else, such as melody (especially striking tunes), tonality (particularly bold modulations), or rhythm.

Of these six basic elements, dynamics and timbre are the two easiest for the beginner to grasp. They are also the least expressly musical: trains are loud, different people have different voices. These two qualities relate more to sound in general than to music in particular.

Chamber music inherently places greater emphasis on purely musical values, and to the extent the beginner needs time to understand what these are, it can be more difficult to listen to. On the other hand, chamber music is actually the best way to hear tonality, rhythm, and melodic development at work since it tends to highlight these elements in the course of the musical argument. Unlike orchestral music, there's no hiding behind harps and horns, cymbals and sixty violins. This is why musical scholars rightly consider chamber music to be the medium through which many composers created their greatest musical legacy, and why composers took up the challenge of concentrating their thought along a more difficult, but fundamentally musical, channel.

As Haydn's example demonstrates, chamber music is often the arena in which great experiments and advances in the art of composition occur. Of course, there's always a practical aspect as well. It's much easier (and cheaper) for a budding musical radical to get four people together than ninety. Our estimate of the significance of many of our greatest masters, Brahms and Fauré, for example, would make no sense without consideration of their contribution to chamber music. Even for a composer such as Mahler, who left nothing mature in this field, his importance lies to a remarkable degree in his development of an orchestral technique that gives every part the same importance as in a chamber work.

Chamber music functions as a musical yardstick, an ideal, and this is the principal source of the "chamber music myth." Its subscribers neglect the obvious fact that the reason we value these compositions so highly is precisely because the musical qualities we hold to be significant are more in evidence, and thus easier to hear in this medium than in any other. Part of the problem is plain snobbery. Chamber music has a reputation for being a performer's medium, designed for a select and highly educated audience.

In the days before recordings the only way to hear music was, naturally, to play it yourself. Orchestral works were available in chamber transcriptions, but even then truly accomplished amateur performers were a tiny minority among the music-loving public. Besides, learning to play an instrument is simply a feat of physical dexterity. It says nothing about intelligence, musicianship, or anything else. We can be very sure that most of the so-called "connoisseurs" of the past were music snobs of average intelligence, who had an additional ability to play an instrument badly.

Today at least most music snobs don't play instruments, which is to their credit, despite the fact that the circumstances of most chamber music recitals make enjoyment virtually impossible. A string quartet in Carnegie Hall, however legendary the acoustics, lacks so much color and impact that only the most determined culture vulture could possibly be expected to stand it. Even smaller halls are often too large to allow a proper sense of dynamics to come through, let alone convey the sense of intimacy with the performers that leaves the listener with a sense of having gotten full entertainment value. This is where recordings come into their own. Chamber music is the ideal medium for home listening. The sense of having the players right in front of you is something recordings do particularly well, and a piano trio in your living room is certainly a more plausible acoustical illusion than a 120-piece orchestra.

Now that we've dispelled some of the intellectual fog surrounding chamber music, let's experience it directly. The three following musical examples demonstrate the three most basic points we can derive from the above discussion:

1. The term *chamber music* implies a limitation only in the number of instruments required, not in the size or scope of the music itself.

2. A composer's style remains recognizable regardless of the medium employed. Chamber music is not some sort of extraordinary aberration of the composer's muse. If you warm to his orchestral stuff, the chamber works will pose no problem.

3. Chamber music represents an opportunity to highlight the most purely musical elements of composition. And while this may require some extra listening, it will reward repetition accordingly.

EXAMPLE I

Haydn: *Symphony No. 94 ("Surprise")*
Haydn: *String Quartet in C, Op. 76, No. 3 ("Emperor")*

Let's compare these two mature Haydn masterpieces one movement at a time, looking for easily audible similarities despite the different forces involved.

First Movements

One of the points we noted in our earlier discussion of both the Baroque concerto and the Classical symphony was that the most highly organized movement tends to be the first, with the others providing a gradual relaxation or release of tension. If so, then these two opening movements appear puzzling. After a brief introduction, the symphony's Allegro sings in a light triple meter. This becomes especially evident in the waltzlike accompaniment to the second subject (played by the violins). Our analysis of Vivaldi's "Spring" taught us that triple meters more frequently suit finales.

Similarly, the quartet's first movement, though written in the more traditional duple meter, develops a strikingly dancelike impetus that becomes a genuine peasant festival, complete with bagpipes, in the development section. Clearly, in these cases, Haydn wishes to minimize the emotional seriousness of his first movements, while retaining the intellectual rigors of sonata form. If the weight of the orchestration is sufficient to ground the lightness of the meter in the symphony, the quartet creates a similar effect out of a slightly heavier rhythm. The stamping peasants make the point more obviously than anything in the symphony. Harmony and rhythm stand in for the comparative lack of sonority, producing moments at least as colorful as anything in the orchestral work.

Second Movements

Haydn's reason for lightening his first movements becomes evident in both cases on hearing the second. Each is a theme and variations in slow tempo that provides the high point of the entire work. The first movements assume, in retrospect, the character of introductions to what follows. Because the theme of the symphony's second movement is a nursery tune of the "Twinkle, Twinkle Little Star" variety, the effect of the variations, to say nothing of the famous surprise, depends entirely on the ability of the orchestra to clothe such simplicity in the widest variety of timbres and dynamics.

For a string quartet, a variation movement based on a tune similar to that in the symphony would be disastrously monochrome. So Haydn doesn't even attempt it. He bases the second movement of the quartet on his "Emperor's Hymn"—better known today as the German anthem, "Deutschland über Alles." What the quartet lacks in terms of sheer color and volume, it more than makes up for in the beauty and solemnity of the melody. Each instrument has a chance to play the tune, and the variations never obscure its nobility and poise. If the effect of the symphony's slow movement is humor tinged with nostalgia, then that of the quartet strikes a deeper note of almost religious reverence.

Third Movements

Both symphony and quartet sport one of Haydn's newfangled minuets, really scherzos in all but name. In his never-ceasing attempt to stay fresh and original, Haydn began speeding up his minuets, as these two examples show. The symphony's third movement gains an extra bit of propulsion through a very strong emphasis on the tune's accompanying waltz rhythm, while the quartet does just the opposite. Here, Haydn feels confident enough in his four players to indulge in some rhythmic tricks that he wouldn't likely risk with a full orchestra.

Fourth Movements

The finales of both pieces present Haydn with a problem of balance. So far, the weight of each piece has been concentrated in the first two movements. While the first movements were clearly introductory, they also employed fully developed sonata forms, however lightly. In the symphony, Haydn again reverses precedent by writing his finale in duple meter. The form is his unique sonata/rondo hybrid, in which the first subject occurs in the home key midway through the development, separating two big developmental episodes. Notice that Haydn adds drama to these episodes by placing both of them squarely in minor keys. This gives his finale a sense of seriousness and depth that along with the "first movement" meter more than offsets the potentially top-heavy structure of the symphony.

The quartet goes one step further than the symphony in having an exceptionally long finale almost entirely in a minor key, and in fully developed sonata form. The music only decides on a happy ending in the last few moments. Emotionally speaking, this stern, at times almost forbidding music greatly outstrips the symphony in sheer intensity. Although both compositions share an almost identical structure—a light opening that introduces a more important slow movement in variation form, then a quick minuet that serves as prelude to a finale with the weight of a first movement—the quartet makes up for its lack of orchestral splendor by emphasizing melody and tonality to a greater degree. The result is a work not only slightly longer than the symphony in terms of sheer duration, but a deeper and more serious composition overall.

EXAMPLE 2

Dvořák: *Symphony No. 7 in D minor*
Dvořák: *Piano Trio in F minor*

Two of Dvořák's minor-key pieces have one thing in common with the Haydn coupling just discussed: the chamber work (for piano with violin and cello) is constructed on an even larger scale than the orchestral composition. This makes sense, given the fact that a medium which has frequent recourse to the most purely musical elements of melody and tonality will need additional time to develop. An orchestra can use its extreme dynamic range and diversity of instruments to create a memorable event within a few bars, while the chamber work may have to create a different mood through modulation to a distant key, or the introduction of a new tune with the necessary emotional qualities. Either option enlarges the form.

Comparison of Haydn's two works stressed the composer's ability to adapt his style to the performing apparatus in order to create virtually identical larger structures with differing emotional qualities. Dvořák does the opposite, deliberately employing different techniques of musical construction to achieve the same, grandly tragic effect. Let's compare once again and see how he does it.

First Movements

For convenience' sake, a simple list of elements common to both movements will clarify their form and content:

1.   Both pieces begin with a mournful, minor-key theme that immediately works up to a stormy and forceful repetition.

2.   Next follows a lyrical second subject in a contrasting major key, also reaching a climax that the return of the first subject immediately contradicts.

3.   Because of internal repetitions of both subjects, and the sense of ongoing development and growth, neither exposition is repeated.

4.   The recapitulation in both movements becomes the logical culmination of the very turbulent development sections, with the first subject appearing fortissimo at the climax.

Now consider the differences:

1.   The symphony's opening bars hardly form a tune; "motif" is a more appropriate word, since all it does is assert an omi-

nous minor key. The piano trio, by contrast, starts with a soulful unison for violin and cello. The full orchestra has the ability to make its brief motif dramatically effective, while the trio relies, as did Haydn in his quartet, on a more lyrical, melodically based style.

2. The first subject of the symphony takes a while to arrive at its initial climax, digressing through a lengthy major-key episode before reappearing as if by surprise. Afterward, however, the opening motif becomes almost ubiquitous, creating a greater and greater sense of thematic concentration. In the trio, just the opposite happens. The first theme recurs frequently, but always with a questioning air, cloaked in strange harmonies that lead to new developments. A large orchestral work has built-in grandeur, and Dvořák's intent is to suggest power and terseness of design. In the trio, he deliberately broadens the pace of the argument to create the expansive sense of scale that the music would otherwise lack.

3. The symphony's first movement ends quietly, in a mood of extreme darkness and exhaustion, the logical reaction against so much taut and strenuous musical striving. Once again the chamber work does the opposite, ending in high rage, also a logical reaction to its first subject's tendency to express resignation and harmonic uncertainty.

Middle Movements

Because Dvořák places the scherzo of his piano trio second, and in the symphony third, with the slow movements located in the third and second positions respectively, we must consider these middle movements as a block. The urgency of the symphony's opening requires a compensating release of tension, hence a major-key slow movement in its customary second position, where it functions quite clearly as an interlude. Plentiful use of flute, clarinet, and horn maintain a rustic, pastoral atmosphere which, though not lacking solemnity, projects a sense of contentment above all else. On the other hand, the slower pace and lyrical indulgence of the trio's first movement prompted Dvořák to increase the musical activity by following it up with the scherzo—no less an interlude in its context than the symphony's Andante.

The symphony's scherzo, like the trio's, tickles the ear by juxtaposing duple and triple meters simultaneously. Its rhythmic energy and minor-key harmonies signal a continuation of the argument begun in the first movement. By the same token the third movement of the trio, a soulful Adagio hovering between major and minor, between smiles and tears, picks up the melodic thread of its work's respective opening measures. Although almost exactly the same length as the symphony's Andante, the trio's slow movement seems longer owing to the slower tempo and broader phrasing. In fact, despite the different positions of the two movements, the contrast between them clearly resembles that noted in Haydn's two works.

Fourth Movements

Both works conclude with minor-key finales that win through to victorious conclusions only at the very end. Your interest should be concentrated on the last few minutes of each movement—the codas in particular. The symphony runs through several abortive attempts to end in the minor, each faster and more desperate than the one preceding, until the orchestra literally wrenches the music around to the major key in a glorious concluding hymn shot through with brazen dissonance. The trio, on the other hand, keeps trying to conclude in the major, only to be cut off by solemn chords and lyrical digressions, the last of which turns out to be the opening tune of the first movement. When this theme finally yields to the major key the piece at last concludes in rousing fashion.

Although the emotions expressed by these two magnificent works are remarkably similar, the pieces are constructed in many ways as mirror images of each other. Dvořák's style remains clearly recognizable throughout; but whereas Haydn bent his orchestral and chamber styles to fit identical formal and expressive molds, Dvořák alters his large-scale organization to give the chamber work the same sense of scope as his symphony. He does this by emphasizing slower tempos and longer melodies capable of richer tonal shadings. This in turn enlarges the form and produces the feeling of "bigness" that the chamber work requires, and which a symphony has almost without trying. In the orchestral medium, his challenge is to create a mood of urgency and concision. That both techniques succeed in producing a uniformly passionate, at times almost tragic atmosphere is one of those wonderful musical facts that make repeated listening with real concentration so endlessly rewarding.

EXAMPLE 3
Beethoven: *String Quartet No. 14 in C-sharp minor*

Now this is really seizing the bull by the horns. Beethoven's late string quartets played a big part in creating the "chamber music myth." Not only have they acquired a reputation for austere sublimity and complexity that makes any rational attempt at understanding (heaven forbid, enjoyment!) utterly futile, they are widely regarded as the most profound statements in all of Western music, period. Just what a pity this perception is you'll come to see as we discuss this great work as a piece of music rather than as a supernatural event.

The quartet consists of seven sections assembled in one large, continuous movement. Musically, the argument is surprisingly easy to follow, though the feelings and emotions that it generates I'm going to leave pretty much up to you to determine. The first section is a slow fugue that wanders through several keys like a conversation in search of a subject. In the next movement, the tempo speeds up and the music begins to take shape as a rondo, but one that remains singularly vague and dreamy. The essence of the musical conflict thus takes shape as a contest between the rhetorical, Baroque-style discussion using contrapuntal techniques such as the fugue, and the more dramatic, tonally based sonata forms represented by the rondo. At this early stage, however, both impulses remain somewhat unformed.

After the rondo, the instruments begin a very short dialogue puctuated by loud outbursts and a final cadenza for solo violin. This is *recitative* (a musical imitation of speech), each player seeming to speak, and the question they seem to be asking is: What do we do next? The answer is an intensification of the quartet's rhetorical side, in the form of a theme and six highly contrasted variations. This long movement is the heart of the quartet, and you should not try to hear the theme in each variation. Rather, Beethoven tries to make the best possible case for the Baroque aesthetic by wringing as much character as possible from each section within the prevailingly slow-to-moderate tempo.

The rapt tranquillity of the variations is rudely shattered by an uproarious scherzo. This movement counterbalances the previous stasis with an atmosphere of frantic activity. The trio section comes around three times, and the general impression is of running faster and faster on a musical treadmill. Aimless scurrying is surely not the answer the piece has been searching for, even though it's one of music's more remarkable properties that it can make the very proposition so delightfully entertaining.

A slow interlude follows the scherzo's gruff admission of defeat, seemingly saying that the rhetorical stance offered by the variations should win by default. Suddenly, the music erupts in the minor and the finale begins. This movement very closely resembles the finale of the Haydn, being a full-blown sonata form that only yields to the major key in the very last bars. In fact, Beethoven's entire quartet bears close comparison to Haydn's, since it begins with a clearly preludial fugue and rondo that throws the musical weight onto a slow theme and variations, as occurs in Haydn's first two movements, only to be followed by a dance that precedes a stern sonata-form finale. Beethoven, however, attempts to integrate the various sections by placing them within the larger framework of a contest between two different types of musical expression. In this particular case drama defeats rhetoric.

This quartet perfectly illustrates the ability of chamber music to grapple with abstract issues—to be music about music. Unfortunately, it's very easy to be intimidated by this tendency, which, since everyone seems to recognize it, ought to be (and is) perfectly comprehensible. As is usually the case with the great musical masterworks, formal experimentation serves to emphasize expressive content. The bold thrust and final victory of Beethoven's last movement would be less satisfying if it wasn't contradicting a clear musical pull in the opposite direction. Understanding is merely a question of learning the language and experiencing it through listening.

Speaking of learning the language, chamber music does have its own terminology, which we should discuss briefly so that you know what to expect. A sonata, for example, usually means a piece for solo piano. Sonatas for other instruments assume the presence of the piano unless otherwise indicated: violin sonata, cello sonata, clarinet sonata all mean the respective instrument with keyboard. The more common chamber ensembles requiring more than two instruments are:

> string trio: violin, viola, cello
> piano trio (often called just plain "trio"): piano, violin, cello
> string quartet (usually called "quartet"): two violins, viola, cello
> piano quartet: piano and string trio
> piano quintet: piano and string quartet
> string quintet: a string quartet with either an extra viola or cello
> wind quintet: flute, oboe, clarinet, bassoon, horn
> string sextet: two violins, two violas, two cellos

Anything in larger numbers or other arrangements will be noted by the composer accordingly.

I hope these examples will lead you to explore the many masterpieces of chamber music contained in Part Two. This medium has languished for too long in the hands of a tiny minority, largely because of serious misconceptions about its difficulty and attractiveness. One final point: the lack of the torrential dynamics and vast contrasts typical of the orchestra make chamber music a very likely candidate for background music, and its effect can certainly be relaxing. I'm not saying that you should never use the classics for this purpose. By all means do so with a clear conscience. But also be aware that some wonderful things await your acquaintance if you're willing to give the music the time and attention that it so richly rewards.

8

▼

Solo Personalities:
The Concerto

ONE OF THE MOST WONDERFUL THINGS
about art is the way in which succeeding generations renew and
reinterpret the ideas of their predecessors. Consider the concerto.
When the sonata style and the symphony swept through the
orchestral universe, solo players didn't just disappear. They still
clamored for repertoire, and composers were happy to oblige. But
the sonata-concerto posed a series of difficult problems that only
Mozart, with his flair for operatic drama, symphonic movement,
and keyboard virtuosity was able to gradually solve in his series of
twenty-seven concertos for piano and orchestra.

We've seen that the entire orchestral revolution inaugurated
by Haydn was aimed at developing an ensemble that could drama-
tize music through the development and interaction of self-con-
tained themes. Imagine then the difficulty of introducing a solo
voice into this scheme. For Haydn and Mozart, it would have been
unthinkable that the orchestra should restrict itself to mere accompaniment and forgo full use of the many new, colorful contrasts
available. What seemed necessary was a form that would allow the
orchestra to display itself to the fullest, without stealing the show

from the soloist. Haydn never addressed this problem with the fullness of his imagination. The orchestra itself was his instrument. But Mozart found salvation in a relatively new idea: the piano concerto.

The keyboard concerto (a composition for any keyboard instrument, from harpsichord to fortepiano to piano) was actually invented by Bach. His treatment of the solo followed the usual Baroque pattern already discussed in Chapter 3. Until that point, the solo instrument of choice had been the violin. (Most of Bach's keyboard concertos are arrangements of works originally composed for violin.) But in order to allow the sonata-orchestra full play, Mozart required a solo voice that could hold its own against the larger ensemble. The recently invented piano was the perfect choice. It offered the singing quality of a string instrument, along with the ability to play massed harmony. It was both forceful enough and versatile enough to give the orchestra a real run for its money. Interestingly, both Haydn and Mozart gave up writing violin concertos at an early age, no doubt because of the limitations they felt this type of solo would have imposed in terms of tone quality and volume. Always remember that in the sonata style failure to take full advantage of the instrumental resources available compromises the music not only technically, but emotionally and expressively since it limits character growth.

Mozart's solution to the problem of a sonata-concerto was as simple in theory as it was subtle in practice. Imagine him addressing his shiny new piano, and saying, "You wish to participate in concert with my magnificent orchestra? Very well. First you must prove yourself worthy of the task by introducing yourself, discussing the terms of your arrangement, and then by standing on your own two feet." Unlike the polite exchanges between solo and orchestra in the concerto grosso, the sonata-concerto is a contest of wills that serves to justify both musically and dramatically the presence of a solo voice within the orchestra as an *equal* partner. Let's look at a sample concerto, one of Mozart's finest, and see how he adapts the sonata style to this new purpose.

Mozart: *Piano Concerto No. 20 in D minor*

The easiest way to understand what goes on in this piece is to return to our exercise in analogous description in the discussion of sonata form. But I'm sick (figuratively at least) of drinks and cookies, and another scenario happens to fit this work especially well. Think of the plot of the classic film *The African Queen.* Call the orchestra Bogart and the piano Hepburn, and summarize the action.

The concerto begins with a portrait of Bogart: tense, wary, but determined. The film takes place during World War I, and a sense of conflict permeates the music. After a lengthy introduction, Hepburn, still in shock from the murder of her missionary brother, quietly pleads for help. Bogart thinks she's crazy, but she uses his own arguments (themes) against him, and they set off together down the river in search of safety. Although he thinks that she's just a timid, inexperienced woman, she eventually wins his respect. So when the introduction returns, the two of them share the material, finally united in their goal. In fact, Bogart's confidence in Hepburn's character has grown to the point where he permits her to pilot the boat herself (a long solo passage called a *cadenza),* before wrapping up the first movement.

The second movement is a quiet interlude of relaxation from the all-pervading menace that threatens the two protagonists. Even under terrible strain and in deadly peril Hepburn and Bogart find romance. ("Romance" happens to be Mozart's title for this movement.) The last movement, a rondo, returns us to the main drama. The *African Queen* is sinking, the companions, now German prisoners about to be executed, say their last goodbyes. Suddenly the German vessel strikes the submerged *Queen* and blows to bits. The bad guys go down with their ship; Bogart and Hepburn react with predictable joy.

Now let's look at the piece a little closer musically and see, point by point, how Mozart's concerto strategy differs from that of a symphony:

1. In a symphony, there's practically no limit on the number or type of characters your drama may employ. Here, however, one character is ready-made by virtue of its solo presence. As with any solo, your ears will tend to concentrate on that voice at the expense of the orchestra. Mozart realizes this, and so gives the first big statement to the orchestra alone. This increases your feeling of expectation, and it forces the solo to adapt itself to the terms set forth by the larger ensemble. Nonetheless, the solo's participation is much more than an addendum to the orchestral introduction, since Mozart saves any change of key until after the presentation of the solo voice. Only after the solo presents its material can the drama begin. In other words, the two *need each other* to go anywhere; the orchestra, and the listener, must wait for the solo to realize the composer's intention.

2. The first movement, unlike most classical symphonies, has no literal repeats. This is because everything is going to get said at least twice anyway by both orchestra and soloist. These movements tend to be long, especially when the solo brings in tow a large number of its own themes. The ongoing effort to justify a solo presence in the orchestra takes time—sometimes a lot of time if they don't get on well and the music is full of conflict and tension.

3. The extreme length of the first movement helps explain why many concertos have only three, instead of four or more. Doubtless you'll come across someone who will tell you that the three-movement concerto is a holdover from the Baroque solo concerto. Don't believe it. Plenty of Baroque concertos have more or fewer than three movements. As you listen, you'll discover that most concertos are at least as long as symphonies, even though they have fewer distinct subdivi-

sions. Overall length and emotional balance are always the real determining factors.

4. The movements following the first take advantage of the cooperation begun there, but have an additional option in that they can focus either on the relationship between solo and orchestra, or on some goal that the pair pursue together. Mozart does both. The important thing to remember is that his sonata-concerto, like *The African Queen,* really contains two simultaneous plot lines.

5. Beware of generalization. No two concertos, even by Mozart, approach the relationship between solo and orchestra in exactly the same way. To prove this to yourself try playing his next one, No. 21 (discussed in Part Two), while thinking about *The African Queen.* You'll get the point.

Mozart's method of creating full characters of *both* the orchestra and soloist became the model for Beethoven and Brahms—but not for too many others. After all, it's much easier to make a movie that has one main character instead of two, and that follows a single plot line. As the idea of a self-supporting orchestra came to be taken for granted, a new concerto idea took hold: let the solo be the only fully developed character. The orchestra can use its resources in providing a background environment and cast of supporting characters against which the solo will react. Because we lose some of the broad alternating contrasts employed in creating the orchestral personality, it will be necessary for the solo to use every technical resource in holding its own against the constantly shifting background. Thus was born still another concerto species—the *virtuoso concerto.*

Weber: *Konzertstück (Concert Piece) in F minor for Piano and Orchestra*

In examining this early example of the "virtuoso" concerto, note first the similarities with Mozart. Both pieces are for piano and orchestra, and both proceed from minor to major—unhappy to happy. But that's about all they have in common. Weber's *Konzertstück* is comprised of four linked sections. And rather than our having to dream up a plot for the drama, the composer himself has supplied one.

A young noblewoman sits on her balcony waiting for her knight to return from the Crusades. Years have passed, and she fears for his life. Her vivid imagination conjures up the horrible deaths that may have overtaken him, and she passes out. End of part one.

As part two begins, our heroine regains consciousness. The sound of a march comes from the distance. She strains to pick out the approaching figure, spots her lover, and jumps up in joy (a *glissando,* or slide, all the way up the keyboard). She runs out to greet him, they embrace ecstatically, and the rest is up to your imagination. Whatever happens, it's pretty vigorous.

As with Mozart, you don't have to know any of this to understand the piece perfectly. What matters is that the piano represents the single protagonist, while the orchestra covers everything else: her visions of horror, the military march, and perhaps even her knight. The march gives the orchestra the opportunity to display its full colors without having to accompany the solo, and for the rest of the time the ensemble happily provides a dramatic foil for her rapidly shifting moods. Of the two, Mozart's is by far the more sophisticated method of approaching the sonata-concerto problem. But Weber hardly lacks drama, and his writing for piano is truly brilliant in a way that Mozart approaches only in his cadenzas (remember? the solos where the orchestra doesn't play).

Here then are two ways of writing concertos for solo with self-supporting orchestra. Mozart's we'll call the "justification" concerto because at some point the soloist will prove himself an equal partner in the collaboration, and because the action of justifying his presence is part of the dramatic point. We called Weber's method the "virtuoso" concerto because the strategy of the piece lies in expressing the range of personality shown by the soloist *against* whatever the orchestra tries to throw at him. One form presents two equal protagonists, the other a single principal character and any number of subsidiary personalities or environments. The remainder of this chapter traces the history of these two forms down to the present in six examples, each containing representatives of the two concerto "schools." I make additional comments where necessary, but as always the real work is up to you.

Justification Concerto: *Beethoven—Violin Concerto*
Virtuoso Concerto: *Mendelssohn—Violin Concerto*

As we saw earlier, violin concertos of the "justification" type are incredibly difficult to write. Beethoven's only stab at this problem resulted in one of his very greatest works. In order to make the soloist at home in his orchestral surroundings, Beethoven endowed his concerto with an almost cosmic serenity and nobility of emotion, then packed it to the gills with absolutely gorgeous, violin-like melodies. When the soloist takes up the tunes, they find fulfillment in being played on the violin.

Mendelssohn begins with his soloist straight away. Notice how much shorter his first movement turns out to be. Beethoven's is almost two-thirds as long as Mendelssohn's entire concerto because the initially timid solo must establish itself in relation to a large orchestra, with its own themes. But Mendelssohn also manages to show off his orchestra in contriving the most vivid and delicate of accompaniments. Listen in both concertos to the ways in which the solo blends with and opposes the woodwind sections as the dramas unfold. Beethoven's wind writing sounds absolutely luminous, while Mendelssohn makes particularly brilliant use of his flutes.

Justification Concerto: *Brahms—Violin Concerto*
Virtuoso Concerto: *Bruch—Violin Concerto No. 1*

Brahms' first movement is one of his richest and most imposing, and is clearly modeled on Beethoven's (preceding example).
Bruch's, by contrast, represents a logical step in the virtuoso process; the entire first movement is nothing but a fiery and passionate
introduction to the beautiful slow movement. Both works conclude
with dazzling rondo-finales in the "Hungarian" style popular at
that time.

Justification Concerto: *Dvořák—Cello Concerto*
Virtuoso Concerto: *Rachmaninoff—Piano Concerto No. 2*

Cello concertos are even harder to write than violin concertos,
since the range of the instrument lies so low and its sound is
therefore easily obscured. Dvořák's mastery of the orchestra is so
complete that for him the problem hardly exists. Notice the way in
which the theme of the opening movement appears just before the
very end of the whole piece—a recollection of past struggles.

The most interesting point about the Rachmaninoff, aside
from its usual fund of shatteringly lovely melody, is the way in
which the piano actually accompanies the orchestra for much of the
time, rather than the other way around. This is, incidentally, one of
his few big works that does not include an obvious reference to the
Dies irae. The tune of the slow movement might sound familiar to
you, but I leave it to you to figure out which pop artist stole it for
his own use.

Justification Concerto: *Elgar—Violin Concerto*
Virtuoso Concerto: *Sibelius—Violin Concerto*

One of the most introverted of all concertos coupled with one of the most extroverted. Elgar's magnificent work throws the weight of the structure onto the finale by letting the solo cadenza in that movement summarize the entire emotional distance that the work has covered in the first two parts. The "justification," therefore, actually occurs in the finale, rather than during the first movement as in the preceding examples. Notice here how the orchestra vibrates sympathetically in the background, actually listening to the solo. The whole piece is a character sketch of one of Elgar's lady friends. Is Elgar himself represented in the orchestra?

Sibelius was himself sort of a closet violinist—not good enough to make it on the virtuoso circuit, so he wrote this kick-ass concerto instead, one of the most brilliant by anybody for anything. The predominantly dark sonority of the orchestra means that every note of the solo stands out. The opening sounds for all the world like a single lonely figure singing alone in a frost-covered forest clearing (at least to me, anyway). However you picture it, the orchestra clearly represents an environment, or even a landscape. The finale alternates uncertainly between major and minor. Listen to how the solo drunkenly totters between the two different modes before making up its mind at the last minute to finish happily.

Justification Concerto: *Nielsen—Clarinet Concerto*
Virtuoso Concerto: *Barber—Violin Concerto*

Perhaps in reading the analysis of Mozart's "African Queen" concerto (don't tell anyone I called it that!), you might have wondered what would happen in a justification concerto where the orchestra and the soloist simply fail to get along. Well, here's your answer. Nielsen's clarinet tries every strategy open to it to convince the small orchestra that it knows what it's doing. At various times the bassoons, horns, and strings seem willing enough to cooperate. But the snare drum won't hear anything of it, and the solo keeps getting furious in a self-defeating sort of way. In the end, orchestra and soloist part company exhausted. Even the snare drum decides to call it a day. Nielsen's sensitivity to musical conflict and drama in the concerto context has given us what might be the greatest concerto written in this century.

Barber's soloist, by contrast, only decides to be a virtuoso in the last movement. The first two movements feature some of the most singing, cozy, and luscious cooperation between solo and orchestra ever conceived. Listen especially to the way in which Barber makes the orchestra continue the soloist's melody at the beginning of the work. It's almost as if they're trying to convince themselves that they're just one huge violin. But the darker emotions hinted at in the first movement, and only fitfully plastered over in the second, lead the solo in the end to renounce a life of narcissistic wallowing and go for the gusto.

Justification Concerto: *Berg—Violin Concerto*
Virtuoso Concerto: *Bartók—Piano Concerto No. 2*

Berg's haunting violin concerto is a musical portrait dedicated "to the memory of an angel." The work depicts the suffering of Manon Gropius, daughter of Alma Mahler and architect Walter Gropius, whose life was tragically cut short by a lengthy and fatal illness. Be forewarned, this is not easy music. It lacks any sense of home key, though melodies are recognizable even on first hearing.

Berg's concerto is in two movements, each having two parts. The first movement contains a portrait of the young Manon, followed by a sketch of the girl caught up in the whirl of youth and life—fragments of waltzes, bustling activity, and perhaps a little flirtatiousness. The second movement begins with a terrifying brass fanfare: the sudden onset of her illness. The music depicts her suffering in a horrifyingly graphic manner leading to a tremendous, convulsive climax. Suddenly, the clarinets play a snatch of a Protestant hymn (or chorale) called "It Is Enough"; the effect is of an organ heard in the distance.

The chorale leads to the second part of the movement: a single slow melody begun by the soloist. The entire string section gradually takes it up until they literally swallow her in sympathy. Her suffering ended, Manon has at last found peace in death, just as the soloist finally achieves unity with the rest of the orchestra. The work ends in calm with a last reference to the opening bars of the first movement.

This concerto is one of the most difficult, moving, and disturbing emotional experiences ever created. If you like musical wallpaper, this is definitely not for you. But if you have the time to spend, and can listen deeply enough to realize that there's more to beautiful music than a pretty tune, then I urge you to give this ultimately uplifting work a try.

Just as Berg wrote an apotheosis of the justification concerto in presenting a personality that comes to accept death, so Bartók summarizes many of the most important aspects of the virtuoso concerto. Here the solo faces each subsidiary instrumental group separately, and only meets the entire orchestra in the finale where its part must reach new heights of virtuosity to keep afloat.

The first movement pits the soloist against the woodwinds, brass, and percussion. The strings are silent. The creepy second movement begins with the strings alone, then features the solo accompanied solely by timpani. A quick scherzo brings everyone together for a moment, but the strings interrupt in a varied reprise of the first part of the movement. Be alert to the subtle differences between the return of this "night music" and its original appearance. The finale is a rondo with episodes based on the thematic material of the first movement. The entire piece is thus musically and orchestrally unified against the soloist at the end. Despite having been challenged with the widest range of characters and environments, the personality of the soloist remains preeminent.

* * *

If, at this point, the distinction between the two types of concerto seems obscure or, even worse, trivial, consider the problem from another angle. Compare Weber's *Konzertstück* to the Berg Violin Concerto. Weber's noblewoman does not change or grow through her experience in the work. She's there from the beginning, and we get to see her reaction to various events. Berg's soloist, however, doesn't only react to the orchestra. In the end, she sings her death song and forces the orchestra to sing along with her. In other words, the solo personality evolves to the point where the orchestra reacts to her as well. They become equal partners musically and emotionally.

So even though the virtuoso concerto, at least externally, seems to give more range for the expression of a solo personality, it is actually the justification concerto that does so. Elgar, Nielsen, and Berg wrote their concertos with the express intention of encapsulating a living character. And life is change, growth, and action —not just reaction. I don't say this in order to knock the virtuoso concerto. I want you to know the difference in terms of what to listen for. Virtuoso concertos are generally easier to take on first hearing; justification concertos tend to reward repetition more and provide the deeper emotional experience. All of them express in one way or another the root meaning of the word "concerto"—to strive together. Think of it that way, and you'll never be lost.

9

▼

Musical Description:
Program Music

THE TITLE OF THIS CHAPTER MIGHT SEEM misleading. After all, the music that we discussed previously was often highly descriptive, and certainly extremely expressive. However, we've also seen that it's very hard to pinpoint exactly what music describes or expresses, even though the emotional meaning impresses itself upon the listener quite clearly, giving rise to some very specific images. And although I'd promised myself I wouldn't use quotations from other sources to help me out (and bore you in the process), I came across one that addresses this particular problem so well that you ought to have it. In 1842, Felix Mendelssohn wrote:

> People usually complain that music is so ambiguous; that it is so doubtful what they ought to think when they hear it; whereas everyone understands words. With me it is entirely the converse. . . . The thoughts which are expressed to me by a piece of music which I love are not too indefinite to be put into words, but on the contrary too definite.

Mendelssohn's statement illustrates perfectly the paradox of musical ambiguity. A piece can mean different things to different people, all of them perfectly clear and correct, and above all inexpressible verbally. This is what scholars and aesthetes call "abstract" music. But composers have always been alert to the fact that music can describe things other than feelings—and concretely too, as we saw in Vivaldi's "Spring." During the late nineteenth century, this led to a veritable war between those who claimed that music should remain abstract, and those who believed music to be naturally descriptive.

The leader of the abstract camp was a Viennese critic named Eduard Hanslick (1825–1904), a perfectly horrible snob whose god was Brahms (whom Hanslick believed to be Beethoven's natural successor, and a guardian of Classical virtue). The head of the opposition was the no less dreadful but vastly more talented Wagner (who believed himself to be Beethoven's successor; in short because in using a chorus in his Ninth Symphony, Beethoven recognized the necessity of words to clarify music's meaning, and thus laid the philosophical groundwork for Wagner's own theory of opera). Nowadays, it's kind of hard to see what they were getting so worked up about, though I won't pretend that the argument is utterly insignificant, philosophically speaking. The essential point that nobody seemed to notice was the fact that, to the extent that the continuo style describes rhetoric (argument) and sonata style, drama, all music is descriptive. This makes perfect sense if we keep in mind the vocal origins of instruments.

Abstract music, then, describes people more often than not, simply through the portrayal of various emotional states. Descriptive, or program, music illustrates anything else. Much of the hysteria generated by the Brahms/Wagner conflict revolved around the question of whether an extramusical explanation was necessary to the understanding of program (descriptive) music. This is a pretty silly issue to get upset about, since any music that is not fundamentally intelligible in its own right will be boring in the extreme, and nobody will ever want to hear it. But the question of intelligibility can be highly subjective, especially when the work in question is new. Consequently, the suspicion in musical circles has always persisted that music with an external plot is somehow inferior to the abstract kind. Whether or not this is true can only be answered on an individual basis.

In order to help you make up your mind, I've put together a group of seven popular objects of musical description. Listening to them will give you an excellent sense of differing compositional styles and approaches to the same ideas. But since argument or character development may not necessarily be the subject of the music, it is very important to realize that the principles of form we've discussed so far may not apply. In other words, the music might be built on musical foundations other than melody (continuo music), or tonality (sonata music). It's up to you to determine the balance of elements comprising the formal makeup of each piece. Because these works all purport to describe something essentially extramusical, you should pay particular attention to timbre—the sound of individual instruments, and orchestration—the way in which the composer writes for his ensemble. Often, instrumental color will be a constructive principle in its own right. You'll have a lot of fun with these in purely sonic terms.

1.   TRAINS
      A.   Honegger: *Pacific 231*
      B.   Villa-Lobos: *Bachianas Brasileiras No. 2*

Honegger's train is a huge metal monster, the music a study in movement. Villa-Lobos gives his a Brazilian folksong to sing, and thus endows the train with more human qualities—kind of a South American "little engine that could."

2.   ROMEO AND JULIET
      A.   Tchaikovsky: *Romeo and Juliet* (symphonic poem)
      B.   Prokofiev: *Romeo and Juliet* (ballet)
      C.   Berlioz: *Romeo and Juliet* (symphony)
      D.   Bernstein: *West Side Story*

The writings of Shakespeare have always been a prime source of musical inspiration. Tchaikovsky's masterpiece is a tone poem in sonata style, as befits a drama. The key elements are: a slow introduction representative of Friar Lawrence, the stormy battle between the Montagues and the Capulets, and the famous love theme that describes Romeo and Juliet. Two combinations of these ideas should strike you as especially significant. First, Friar Lawrence vainly attempts to impose peace on the warring families; second, note the way in which the battle finally overwhelms the two lovers. It's not necessary to know the action of the play in detail to follow the course of the music.

Prokofiev's version of the story is a ballet, and a grand spectacle on stage, though the music stands on its own away from the theater. There are several suites floating around that feature many of the best bits. If you get a recording of one of these, be sure that it includes the Balcony Scene, but I recommend hearing it complete. This preserves the narrative order of the music. As in most ballets, the music falls into a series of set "numbers" that move the action along. Don't expect the continuity of Tchaikovsky's version.

Berlioz calls his *Romeo and Juliet* a "dramatic symphony," and uses soloists and a chorus to illustrate the concept of love as portrayed in Shakespeare's play. He basically sets what interests him in the original in terms of musical potential, including several scenes that are of only marginal dramatic interest. With Berlioz, music, as opposed to the play's dramatic narrative, always comes first, as is only fitting. Snotty critics are always the first to gripe about his manhandling of Shakespeare in order to make an effective musical scheme. These are the same folks who then bemoan the "formlessness" of music that slavishly adheres to an unmusical scenario without making the necessary changes. We, however, can enjoy Berlioz's terrific symphony at face value, including the upbeat ending.

West Side Story is of course a modern version of *Romeo and Juliet.* Compare this with the other examples. Listen to the elements in common: love, conflict, grief, and death. To what extent do you think that the music in all four works reflects the original? Can you think of any other ways in which the story might be approached musically?

3.   WATER
   A.   Debussy: *La Mer*
   B.   Rimsky-Korsakov: *Schéhérazade*
   C.   Bridge: *The Sea*
   D.   Britten: *Four Sea Interludes* from *Peter Grimes*
   E.   Sibelius: *The Oceanides*
   F.   Bax: *Tintagel*
   G.   Mendelssohn: *The Hebrides (Fingal's Cave)* (Overture)
   H.   Dvořák: *The Water Goblin*
   I.   Respighi: *The Fountains of Rome*
   J.   Holst: Ballet Music from *The Perfect Fool*

Water has always been a prime source of musical inspiration. A–G all deal with the sea. The Debussy and Rimsky-Korsakov works are probably the classics of this watery genre. Bridge and Britten were teacher and pupil, respectively; both portray the sea's various moods, from calm and quiet to turbulent. Sibelius evokes the seas of Greek mythology; Mendelssohn and Bax both sketch the windswept coast of the British Isles. Dvořák describes a nasty underwater creature who kidnaps a village girl and forces her to bear his child, with tragic consequences. Respighi's lovely tone poem is self-explanatory, but Holst's spirit of water is a liquid, dewy creature of delicate droplets—one of the most haunting aquatic evocations.

4.   FIRE
   A.   Tippett: *Ritual Dances* from *The Midsummer Marriage*
   B.   Wagner: *Magic Fire Music* from *Der Ring des Nibelungen*
   C.   Holst: *Ballet Music* from *The Perfect Fool*
   D.   de Falla: *El Amor Brujo*
   E.   Liszt: *Dante Symphony*

F.   Tchaikovsky: *Francesca da Rimini*
G.   Ruggles: *Sun-Treader*

The first trio of examples all come from operas. Three of Tippett's four dances describe the pursuit of the male by the female, and the second dance (in which a female otter hunts a fish) might just as well belong in the section on water. The fourth, "The Dance of Fire in Summer," is a wild bacchanal (see "Orgies" below) in which the passions of the participants rise as the orchestra flickers like flame. Both Holst's and Wagner's fires similarly concentrate on the idea of flames, though Wagner's are far less rambunctious.

El Amor Brujo (Love, the Magician) is a ballet with songs. It contains the famous Ritual Fire Dance, while other sections found their way onto Miles Davis's famous album *Sketches of Spain*. The action tells the story of a girl haunted by the jealous ghost of her dead lover. It is a really gorgeous work.

Both Liszt and Tchaikovsky tackle one of the most popular sources of fire—hell—as described by that region's great tour guide, Dante. Liszt takes on the whole inferno, then moves to paradise, while Tchaikovsky describes an unfortunate couple that Dante met on one of his visits.

Have you ever imagined what it must sound like to walk on the face of the sun? Well, here's your chance. As you might imagine, the feeling is not comfortable at all, but it sure is intense. Ruggles' wonderful work is not all that hard to follow, but the actual sounds themselves have a searing, coruscating brilliance that more than any other piece I know toys with the boundaries between pleasure and pain.

5.   LIGHT
A.   Tippett: *Ritual Dances* from *The Midsummer Marriage*
B.   Grofé: *Grand Canyon Suite*
C.   Grieg: *Peer Gynt Suite*
D.   Strauss: *Also Sprach Zarathustra*
E.   Haydn: *The Creation*
F.   Druckman: *Aureole*

As a prelude to his set of dances, Tippett's orchestra magnificently describes the midsummer sun bursting through the clouds. The very opening sounds for all the world like butterflies dancing in sunbeams. Do you agree?

Grofé, Grieg, and Strauss all evoke the dawn in creating their musical pictures of light. *Also Sprach Zarathustra* (Thus Spoke Zarathustra) was the source of the famous theme from *2001: A Space Odyssey*. Notice the contrast between music symbolic of darkness and the increasing movement that heralds the approach of day.

It should come as no surprise by now that Haydn, the pioneer of the modern orchestra, was also one of the first and greatest to take advantage of its descriptive possibilities. *The Creation* is an oratorio—a sort of opera designed for concert performance. Since it has a text, you get descriptions of all sorts, the first of which is the separation of light from chaos. Then follows sunrise, moonrise, the creation of animals, and of man. The work is structured by alternating arias (songs) and choruses, which are introduced by a kind of sung speech called *recitative*.

Jacob Druckman's *Aureole* concentrates on a musical description of light's tangible qualities, rather than its manifestation in the natural world. The music pulsates, shimmers, and glitters in an atmosphere tinged with a mysterious luminescence. Although the work is a sort of theme and variations, it's better to ignore the infrequent melodic suggestions and listen to the music as pure texture.

6.   ORGIES
  A.   Tchaikovsky: *Manfred Symphony*
  B.   Wagner: *Venusberg Ballet* from *Tannhäuser*
  C.   Holst: *Choral Symphony*
  D.   Saint-Saëns: *Bacchanale* from *Samson and Delilah*
  E.   Ravel: *Daphnis et Chloé*
  F.   Berlioz: *Symphonie fantastique*
  G.   Berlioz: *Harold in Italy*

Orgies have always been very popular, both with composers and their audiences. This is probably because you can leave most of the sordid detail to the imagination while writing lots of wild, steamy music. Generally speaking, musical orgies come in four varieties: Greek, infernal (as in hell), pagan (but not Greek), and criminal. The above list gives you samples of all four types.

Manfred is Tchaikovsky's greatest orchestral work. The finale of this four-movement symphony is an infernal orgy of the juiciest kind. Wagner's is a Greek bacchanal, though he moved Venus's grotto to Germany for the purpose. But really, whoever heard of a Teutonic orgy? In his opera *Tristan and Isolde,* Wagner had killed off the heroine with a monumental psychosomatic musical orgasm induced by the mere sight of her lover's corpse. After that, group sex was a piece of cake, especially since he could pawn the whole thing off as concession to the French production. As you will see below, the French are without a doubt specialists in this sort of thing.

Holst's Choral Symphony, as befits a work based on the poetry of Keats (including the "Ode on a Grecian Urn") is more of an aesthetic orgy than anything else, though the first movement features a genuine bacchanal in the classic sense. The best part of this wonderful work, however, is the light and breezy scherzo. You're in for a real treat here, especially if you follow the words closely. And now to the real experts.

Saint-Saëns' bacchanal is a pagan orgy, after which, in the complete opera, Samson rips down the Philistines' temple and kills everyone. He's angry at not having been allowed to participate. Ravel's tussle is probably the most graphic of them all. Be sure to get a recording of the complete ballet. That way, you get the chorus parts, which are especially essential at the orgasmic conclusion of the work. No words, just lots of appropriately ecstatic moaning.

From Berlioz, two sensational examples. The *Symphonie fantastique,* a musical portrait of a drug-induced stupor, concludes with a truly hellish witches' Sabbath based on our friend the *Dies irae.* This is the last hallucination in a series that has already included visions of a ball, a day in the country, and the subject's own execution. The

"Orgy of Brigands" from *Harold in Italy,* by contrast, hardly includes the title character at all. Harold is much better at suicide than the hero of the *Fantastique,* and dies before things really heat up.

7.   SPACE
    A.   Williams: *Star Wars*
    B.   Vaughan Williams: *Sinfonia Antartica*
    C.   Holst: *The Planets*

By definition, space is the ultimate in emptiness. It is therefore essential that a musical depiction of it leave out anything that smacks of humanity. Listen to these examples with an ear to the harmonic, melodic, rhythmic and, above all, textural qualities that yield a sense of remoteness and isolation.

John Williams' brilliant music to *Star Wars* is a modern example of what was called in the last century *incidental music:* music written to accompany stage action. He combines instrumental textures representing space with the surging, vocal melodies of the human protagonists. Vaughan Williams' symphony was also assembled from film music, and depicts the struggle of man against the elements (the film, *Scott of the Antarctic,* describes the famous explorer's tragic final expedition). Note his use of wordless voices to give the music an *inhuman,* otherworldly character. Although technically not about space, the music evokes a similarly hostile, alien environment in which man is a stranger.

Holst's *The Planets* is the classic source of all subsequent space music. He composed it as far back as 1915, and it's a wonderful example of non-sonata construction. The suite is in seven movements, with Jupiter (No. 4) acting as the focal point of the piece. On either side of this fulcrum the remaining six movements balance, antithetical images of each other: 1. Mars (Motion [Rhythm]) —7. Neptune (Stasis); 2. Venus (Sublime)—6. Uranus (Vulgar); and 3. Mercury (Lightness)—5. Saturn (Heaviness). Holst thus achieves a coherent whole organized around rhythm, tempo, and texture without relying on long-term melodic or tonal strategies.

*   *   *

As you go through these pieces, it may become apparent to you why descriptive music has caused critics and scholars so much difficulty. Simply put, the modern orchestra became so flexible and the sources of musical inspiration so varied that many of these pieces cannot be pigeonholed and placed in larger structural categories. When critics can't say that a piece is written along some strictly predetermined pattern, they call it "formless." But as we've seen, even supposedly fixed formal concepts are actually quite free. That is why you must listen to each work individually, and discover its structure for yourself. Preconceived notions of form will only prevent understanding. Many of the most famous musical scholars and critics have often been very lazy listeners.

10
▼

Musical Meaning:
The Three Basic Kinds of Musical Expression

IF IT WERE POSSIBLE TO ACTUALLY DESCRIBE music with words, then music would be unnecessary. Nevertheless, it's only natural that we should try to interpret our experiences and feelings with language, our most specific means of communication. The terms we defined in discussing continuo and sonata music exist because so many works fit each style. When this happens, a vocabulary evolves that helps explain the musical processes at work. Far from being cold and abstract, we've seen that melodically and tonally based music does indeed have a subject: people—talking, arguing, living, and growing. It therefore makes sense that we should be most understandable when we describe something that represents our own feelings and emotions.

When we looked at program music in the last chapter, we discovered that musical instruments naturally lend themselves to the depiction of things that are nonhuman. But this use of music is so extraordinary that most composers feel the need to give the listener a clue as to what they wish to illustrate. The simplest way to do this, as Haydn showed in *The Creation*, is to use words that make the meaning of the music clear. Otherwise, general titles suffice, with the details left to your imagination. In this concluding section of Part One, we will look at the logical culmination of these ideas: music that is impersonal and nonspecific (that is, abstract but not about people).

Up to now, we've introduced many new and difficult terms in a very short space of time. "Impersonal music" is the last, and perhaps the most confusing to the beginner. It's a term I coined to describe a whole range of music that falls outside of the more commonly recurring forms. And there's lots more of it than you might at first think; so before we go on, remember that all music uses all of the possible elements of expression in some form or another. Continuo music didn't ignore tonality, it simply wasn't based on it. Contrast, the very lifeblood of music, is most effective when the qualities in question are in close proximity. Consequently, when speaking of nonhuman, or impersonal, music, keep in mind that works of this type will include much that *is* profoundly human. These compositions use melody; they change key. Arguments arise, and dramatic surprises occur. But these are not the foundations upon which the music is built. In the end, human beings may not win out. I don't mean that anyone dies. It's just that people, or their emotions, aren't the focus of attention.

The works that we'll examine in this chapter will employ both personal and impersonal musical forms. Because no general descriptive vocabulary exists that defines impersonal music, you'll have to use all of your listening powers to discover the form for yourself in these cases. We'll alternate musical examples of both types, and conclude with two examples that employ a musical synthesis of the two ideas in a dramatic, symphonic framework. Of course, you'll have my own fumbling efforts to guide you, and I think you'll find most of this music marvelous, impressive, even delightful. If we're lucky, by the end of the chapter we'll be able to say something intelligent about our ability to find meaning in music.

Monteverdi: *Combattimento di Tancredi e Clorinda*

From the dawn of the continuo period comes *The Battle between Tancredi and Clorinda*. This is one of the most descriptive and personal pieces of music ever written. The plot tells the story of the knight Tancredi, who comes across a woman, Clorinda, disguised as another knight. Tancredi challenges Clorinda to battle, kills her, finds out she's a woman, and has a fit of remorse. The music is entirely the slave of the text. Listen to the stalking rhythm of Clorinda's walking, the sound of Tancredi's pursuit on horseback, their slow circling about each other, and their fighting "like two jealous bulls in a rage." After Tancredi strikes Clorinda down, the music shifts, from describing concrete things, to *emotions:* principally grief and sorrow.

The entire vocal line of this piece rises and falls with the cadence of speech. There is very little "singing," only rhythmic recitation (recitative). Monteverdi's entire aim is to demonstrate the ability of music to heighten the meaning of the words by amplifying their emotional content. The style he opposed can be heard in the next example.

Tallis: *Spem in alium*

This magnificent work is a *motet* (a choral work on a sacred text), traditionally sung *a cappella* (without instruments). This particular setting is for forty independent parts divided into eight five-part choirs. As you may imagine, the text is virtually unintelligible under the circumstances. But don't let that discourage you from listening. Before Monteverdi and his compatriots began to establish instrumental music, all of the most highly developed pieces were written for voices alone. The period before the advent of the continuo was known as "the Golden Age of music," and listening to this work explains why.

Rather than concern himself with the meaning of specific words, Tallis has tried to embody the spirit of religious transcendence. The music seems to float in a timeless void: an effect achieved through a perfectly even, flowing rhythm that only becomes firm at major climactic points. Unlike Monteverdi, who set his text as closely as possible to the natural inflections of speech, Tallis negates every impulse toward straight declamation. In this way, his voices sound like a celestial choir. The music makes its effect through vocal orchestration—the mass and density of the various choirs as they merge and diverge.

This is the first of our impersonal works. The spirit of sacred music requires the expression of something more than mortal. Using only voices, Tallis achieves the tour de force of a composition that sounds superhuman. This is music as sophisticated as any, within its stylistic limitations, and so colorful as to render the mere thought of instruments superfluous.

Bloch: *Schelomo (Solomon)*

Bloch's "Hebraic Rhapsody for Cello and Orchestra" is a musical portrait of King Solomon. Obviously, this is a personal piece, since it evokes a human being. The cello represents the title character, while the orchestra depicts his environment, giving us a virtuoso concerto. Listen at the very beginning to the writing for the solo. When Monteverdi set his text, he used recitative in order to preserve the character of speech. Bloch writes in similar fashion for the cello. The actual words are up to your imagination, but Solomon seems to speak to us through the instrument. This is one way to endow music with human personality.

Sibelius: *Tapiola*

Tapio is the Finnish god of the northern forests, and Tapiola is his home. His spirit permeates the trees, the snows, rivers, and glades. Unlike Schelomo, Tapio is supernatural, nonhuman. Sibelius's music correspondingly avoids any lapse into dramatic or rhetorical expression. The work consists of a series of slowly changing orchestral textures, over which thematic fragments hover and chase each other about. Notice the way in which Sibelius avoids writing melodies that fall into the natural rhythm of speech. All the tune fragments this piece develops are either much slower or much faster than the average pace of words. And their rhythms are very different, too. The storm that develops toward the end is a thrilling and frightening exercise in pure musical texture.

Sibelius: *Pohjola's Daughter*

This composition is an excellent comparison with both *Schelomo* and *Tapiola*. Compare Sibelius's opening to Bloch's. Both begin with a solo cello seeming to speak. In Sibelius's case, this might represent storytellers sitting around a fire recalling mythological events. One instrument after another takes up the narrative in the repeated-note formulas that indicate instrumental speech, until at last they become background to the story itself. Pohjola's daughter sits spinning at her wheel. A great hero with a long unpronounceable Finnish name announces his arrival in the brass, and tries to win her hand by performing the impossible tasks she sets for him. Finally, he gives up in frustration, and the characters vanish into their mythological past. It's drama this time, with two main characters in a sonata movement. Compare the differences in these clear-cut themes and speech sequences with the technique employed in *Tapiola*. And yet, we have no doubt that both pieces are by Sibelius.

Janáček: *Sinfonietta*

No program here, though the composer did suggest titles for the movements which are about as unhelpful as possible. Janáček made a study of the inflections of spoken Czech, out of which he formed his mature musical style. It consists of little more than a mosaic of melodic fragments constantly repeated in ever changing patterns. The music sings, dances, and sounds as articulate and alive as speech: vibrantly, passionately human.

Bruckner: *Symphony No. 5*

Now that you have a sense of the various ways in which music can embody both personal and impersonal qualities, it's time to look at a totally abstract work in which the nonhuman triumphs. Bruckner's Fifth is one of the greatest monuments to pure sound ever erected. Instead of the usual sonata drama, Bruckner's music grows out of the conflict between mortality and spirituality. Bruckner was a devout Catholic. For him, life on this earth was a prelude to existence after death. It is this belief that his music affirms.

First Movement

The work begins with an introduction containing three elements: a slow mass of string harmony over plodding, plucked basses, a huge upward thrust by the whole orchestra, and a chorale, or hymn, in the brass instruments. Never before has music depended so much on the specific sound of instrumental textures. It would be inconceivable to sing this opening, or play it on a piano. Repetition of these motives leads to a huge climax, and the beginning of the Allegro. This consists of three different tune complexes. The first is a heroic theme that always comes up short, the second a slow, faltering passage featuring violins accompanied by plucked strings. The third is a joyful song in the woodwinds that eventually penetrates the whole orchestra, then stumbles and falls down into silence.

The general sense of this movement is clear: three nonhuman elements and three human ones alternate with each other, but almost never directly interact. The human elements fail to maintain their momentum for long, and the motives of the introduction seem monolithic, and utterly impassive. Finally, the heroic theme of the Allegro manages to get up enough energy to bring the movement to a close. Bruckner has presented the subjects of his musical discourse, but has yet to weld them together into a convincing whole.

Second and Third Movements

Bruckner's slow movements always sound special, because they are the most vocal and singing portions of his symphonies; for that reason they communicate more deeply and directly than his quicker movements. The present example is no exception, beginning with a desolate strain on the oboe, and followed by a thrilling, warm answer featuring the full string section.

The scherzo takes the accompaniment to the oboe's lament and turns it into the mechanical motion of a scampering child's toy. Bruckner counteracts the human passion of his Adagio with shadowy games. Bits of dance music flit by. Tunes appear and vanish into thin air. The middle section (trio) does nothing to alleviate the mysterious, supernatural atmosphere that hovers over the music.

Finale

The finale must integrate and reconcile the opposing human and nonhuman elements presented thus far. The movement opens like the very beginning of the symphony, and each movement briefly passes by in review as Bruckner reminds us of the issues left unresolved. The clarinet rejects these recollections with a humorous shrug. Suddenly, the basses take the shrug and begin to argue over it, starting a strenuous fugue. Bruckner recognizes this argument for the futile exercise that it is, for it breaks off as if to say, "If you want to be human, then *sing,* dammit!" So he follows his fugue with a gorgeous passage in which the whole orchestra comes alive with song: not a genuine lyric melody, but an entire texture of singing. The brass instruments rebuke this harshly in a heavy unison passage based on the clarinet's shrug, and accompanied by striding strings.

So far, this movement has paralleled the first in giving us three distinct human elements: an argument, a song, and a shout of indignant frustration. But notice that Bruckner has yet to introduce his nonhuman forces. After the brass and strings quiet down, salvation appears in the form of yet another chorale: stately and resplendent. The strings answer each phrase with hushed awe. But no sooner do they take up the tune of the chorale than they begin another argument (fugue). And as if to prove that all such discussions are similarly futile, this second fugue leads by imperceptible degrees back to the first one, and the two disputes combine furiously.

The resumption of the first debate pushes the music back to square one. All thoughts of heaven vanish. The orchestra once again attempts to sing, only to be confronted once again by the stentorian brass. But this time, the heroic theme from the first movement tries to shout down this spirit of negation. The two themes start a veritable war that proceeds in three stages: violent, mysterious and agitated, then even more tumultuous. Suddenly the chorale blazes out in the brass and covers everything in its glory. The entire orchestra erupts in response and the heroic theme finds fulfillment with the chorale, eternal life the reward for its earthly struggles. Even the indifferent clarinet shrug provides, at last, an affirmative rhythmic impetus.

Bruckner's musical technique has made him one of the most misunderstood composers of all time. Believe it or not, the Wagnerian side of the Brahms/Wagner battle actually chose Bruckner as "their" symphonist, though his music is actually even less clearly descriptive than Brahms'. The only resemblance between Bruckner and Wagner lies in the heroic treatment of the brass instruments, and the very slow pacing. If you really want to blow your mind, listen again to Brahms' Fourth and consider that his orchestra is actually larger than Bruckner's, even though the latter's sounds vastly bigger. Bruckner's orchestra is not a human voice, but a superhuman one. His gaze is not on this life, but on the world beyond.

How are we to describe the process that governs the formal structure of this incredible symphony? Both tonality and melody have their place in Bruckner's scheme. But the essence of Bruckner's style, as with Sibelius's, lies in his extraordinary use of rhythm, timbre, and dynamics to create a series of textures that overwhelm the human musical elements. The process is not dramatic; it's transcendental, much as in Tallis's motet.

Lutoslawski: *Symphony No. 3*

This work is a logical successor to Bruckner's symphony, even though it was composed in 1983—over a hundred years later. The work is in two connected movements. Like Bruckner's first movement, Lutoslawski's consists of several attempts to get started. The four-note "shove" that begins the piece keeps prodding an orchestra that responds with decreasing interest. Finally, with the help of brass and a chime, the second movement starts with—you guessed it—a fugue of sorts. In this case, however, the argument seems welcome after the inactivity of the first part. The entire second movement can be seen as a gradual attempt to put together a sustained passage of song. Each attempt runs into trouble: the music disintegrates into random noises, purely textural roadblocks, and other hazards. Finally after what sounds like a final defeat, the orchestra gathers itself together and at last achieves melody, and the sound of bells carries it higher and higher into the heavens before the four-note shove that started the work slams it home to the finish.

Although you may not detect singable tunes in a work so heavily based upon texture, you should be able to hear the resemblance in technique between Lutoslawski and Bruckner. Only with Lutoslawski, humanity seemingly wins out in the end. No matter how difficult it may sound at first, remember that familiarity will bring understanding and pleasure. I must say in all fairness though, as with the Berg Violin Concerto, if pretty tunes are a must, this symphony is not for you. Otherwise, give it a try. It's worth it.

With this chapter, we've come to the end of a long journey. Although we've seen that instrumental music can be very ambiguous in meaning, it can also be highly specific. As a means of communication, it can express anything that the human spirit can encompass. By emphasizing the inherently vocal qualities of the instruments, composers can depict people and human emotion. When they use instruments descriptively, they can portray in music the world around us. And when composers deliberately and systematically deny their instruments vocal and descriptive characterization, then they can clothe in sound *ideas* and *concepts* that exist only in the mind.

But verbal description such as this has its limitations. I have been intentionally vague about music and the transcendental, and for good reason. If we didn't know that Tapio was a pagan god, and that Bruckner was a Roman Catholic, would we be able to link our perception of the nonhuman in music to the composer's specific creed? I strongly doubt it. Similarly, Lutoslawski's impersonal elements are obstacles to be overcome, while Bruckner's are glorious hymns of affirmation. Meaning depends on content, and the emotional significance of the music depends entirely upon you.

If you failed to hear the human tragedy of Brahms' Fourth, or the spiritual victory in Bruckner's Fifth, the important thing is to feel confident that you've heard *something,* however indescribable. Always ask yourself, What musical elements does the composer highlight, and what does this mean to my interpretation of the music? Never forget the relationship between voices and instruments; this will help you to hear the music tell its story. Don't be afraid to form opinions—and, more important, don't be afraid to change your mind. It's very difficult to talk about something that may never appear the same to you on successive hearings, and it's even harder to write about it. Any statement that I have made so far will be plain nonsense unless you have heard what I'm describing, and I can't take that for granted.

I wish it were possible to summarize the forms of musical language in simple and elegant prose. But I don't think I can do it. Music is not a tidy subject and, like English, many of its constructions are irregular. If hearing this music leads you to question some of your beliefs about art, culture, society, or yourself, then you're listening in the proper spirit. As I said in my introduction, this book is not just about music, it's also about thinking. Understanding a composer's vision presupposes a mind open to differing points of view. Musical form provides only the framework for this vision. That's why generalized formulas are so dangerous. No two works are identical. Form and content are indivisible, and the greatest enemy of art is complacency.

Part II

▼

The Master's Voice

Introduction

IN PART ONE, YOU GRAPPLED WITH THE difficult question "How do I listen?" Now it's time to tackle a much easier issue: "What do I want to listen *to?*" Even though you now have a good sense of how music operates, the sheer scale of available choice can be daunting. Let's hope that the range of examples discussed in Part One has already alerted you to composers whose musical languages you find appealing. You should start listening to a wide range of their works. Beyond this point, however, lie uncharted waters, and even though much of the joy of listening lies in discovery, random selection often leads to disappointment. What you need is a set of criteria for making intelligent choices about what you wish to explore, and—would you believe it?—I just happen to have a few points along these lines for your perusal:

Personal Preference. The single most important consideration in choosing a piece of music is that you should be disposed to like it. You may not love everything about it on first listening, but there should be something enjoyable in it that will justify repeated attention.

Time. In order to avoid boredom or discouragement, you

should arrange your choices so that you get the most out of the time you spend.

Feasibility. Let's face it. There's much more music out there than anyone can cover, even if we limit ourselves to the instrumental repertoire. Omnibus repertoire surveys do exist (remember the guy with the harp, saying "I'm sure you'll recognize this lovely melody as 'Stranger in Paradise' "?), but the essentially random, encyclopedic approach is the exact antithesis of what we're shooting for. In this half of the book, we need to be practical and allow for maximum choice in a minimum amount of verbal space, while still presenting the music meaningfully.

Fortunately, a solution does exist that satisfies these criteria. Otherwise, I wouldn't have bothered you with them in the first place.

You will recall that in Part One, we discussed the problem of describing verbally what happens in music. We overcame this handicap by arranging the musical examples as a series of comparisons that allowed you to hear different approaches to similar subjects, like concertos, program music, etc. Well, by applying this comparative method systematically, you can develop a blueprint of the repertoire that will allow you to plan your musical time efficiently, solely according to your personal tastes and preferences.

First let's take a group of pieces—four, say—and organize them according to a consistent strategy:

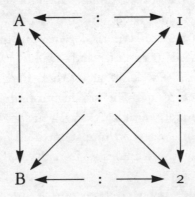

This arrangement yields six possible types of comparison, but we don't have to use all of them. Three will serve as standards, with additional combinations as necessary. So, what we get is A:B, A:1, B:2, and we must decide what these three basic comparisons represent.

Since one of our principal goals is to learn to recognize and understand each composer's unique voice, let A:B compare two works, by two composers, written at about the same time. This allows you to put the music in a certain context, and to note similarities and differences in the styles of contemporaneous musicians. If A and B are by the *same* composer, then you should listen to changes or developments in that composer's personal language. A:B comparisons help you to follow your interest in a given period or style.

We can extend our understanding even further if, as we did in Part One, we look for continuities in musical practice beyond a single period. So let A:1 and B:2 take some aspect of form, content, or technique and show it at work during an earlier or later period, or within different styles. Since there are only a few fundamental elements underlying all musical thought, A:1 and B:2 comparisons permit you to explore music according to type. Instead of listening primarily for variations within a given compositional practice, you will focus on the continuities in our musical tradition that transcend stylistic barriers.

The remainder of this book consists of 88 comparison groups of 352 compositions. Some of them will be familiar from Part One, and many composers appear more than once in different contexts. Just as many will probably be unfamiliar to you, since variety is one of my prime objectives here. All you have to do is find something that you like, and follow the comparisons as your own interests lead you from one rewarding listening experience to another. The pieces you know and love will introduce you to others which, because they employ similar ideas or styles, you will also enjoy. Listen at your own pace, following your own taste. Feel free to explore the widest range of a composer's output after you've been introduced, then come back when you want something new. You will never lack for a pleasurable discovery, or find yourself adrift on an endless ocean of available repertoire.

To help you get started, I have prepared two sample groups for you to try out, if you wish. As with everything in this book, this is entirely optional. You can also select any composer or work from the index, or from Part One, and take it from there. I offer these introductory samples merely to make a few points about the numbered groups.

SAMPLE GROUP I

A. Dvořák: *Serenade for Strings, Op. 22 (1875)*
B. Dvořák: *Serenade for Winds, Op. 44 (1878)*
1. Bartók: *Divertimento for Strings (1939)*
2. Janáček: *"Mladi" (Youth)—Wind Sextet (1924)*
AB A1 B2 12

These three Eastern European composers were all influenced by folk music, yet all sound distinctive. Compare the two Dvořák works (AB), listening to the ways in which he works with string orchestra, and then wind orchestra. The graceful strings waltz and sing, while the more pugnacious winds march with raucous abandon in a more popular vein. Next compare Dvořák with Bartók (A1), noting the differences between the folk inflections of Hungary (Bartók) and Czechoslovakia (Dvořák) within the context of writing for strings. Now listen to the two Czechs (B2), and consider Janáček's relation to his older countryman as they both write for winds alone. Notice that both write marches and share a certain "outdoor" quality. Finally, you might also want to compare Bartók and Janáček (12), who in this context sound more different from each other then either does from Dvořák. Is choice of instruments more important than individual style?

SAMPLE GROUP 2
A. Hindemith: *"Mathis der Maler" Symphony (1934)*
B. Respighi: *Church Windows (1922–25)*
1. Vaughan Williams: *Job—A Masque for Dancing (1930)*
2. Martinů: *The Frescoes of Piero della Francesca (1955)*
AB A1 B2

Here are four examples of symphonic painting. Hindemith's symphony illustrates three panels from the Isenheim Altarpiece of Matthias Grünewald. Vaughan Williams designed his ballet along lines suggested by William Blake's *Illustrations to the Book of Job*. Respighi's piece is self-explanatory, as is the Martinů. But here's the interesting point. As you compare, you will probably find that Respighi and Martinů sound more obviously colorful and descriptive than Hindemith and Vaughan Williams. Actually, in terms of compositional intent, the opposite case obtains. The titles in *Church Windows* were given after the composition of the music and are not even entirely the composer's. Martinů's frescoes illustrate mood more than specific images, and the last movement actually combines two different scenes. The reason for this apparent anomaly is not hard to discern. Orchestral color plays a much more important role in the styles of Martinů and Respighi than in Hindemith or Vaughan Williams, who, in developing their musical materials at greater length, sound somehow more symphonic throughout.

In fact, both of these sample comparisons demonstrate that a composer's individual voice remains distinctive despite any larger group or school to which he supposedly belongs. Dvořák, Janáček, and Bartók share clearly audible characteristics derived from folk music, and yet retain unique personalities. Hindemith, Vaughan Williams, and Respighi all wrote their pieces within the same decade, and on biblical subjects at that. They all make reference to medieval or ancient music, while remaining true to themselves.

Martinů, writing in a thoroughly modern style, somehow manages to sound the most mysterious and legendary of all.

The art of listening to the great classics rests, at least partly, on two balancing precepts. You must try to find continuity, to relate similar ideas and images, without losing your appreciation of each composer's contribution to and interpretation of the larger whole of our musical tradition. You now have all the tools you need to participate in and enjoy this great heritage. In fact, you've had the ability all along. I hope I've been able to help you recognize this fact. So get going, and happy listening!

GROUP I
A. Haydn: *Symphony No. 102 (1795)*
B. Mozart: *Symphony No. 40 (1788)*
1. Prokofiev: *Classical Symphony (1917)*
2. Schubert: *Symphony No. 5 (1816)*
AB A1 B2

Haydn and Mozart frequently sound very similar to casual listeners, but this comparison lets you hear the wide range of music they created within the context of the Classical symphony. Essentially, Mozart prefers long-breathed melodies and warm colors, while Haydn likes to work with sharp, rhythmically distinct motifs. Haydn's orchestrations usually put instrumental clarity ahead of blended sonorities.

Prokofiev's Classical Symphony is more than a mere spoof. It recaptures the wit and humor of Haydn in contemporary terms. Compare especially the two finales, both models of brevity and charm. Schubert's Fifth, though in a major key as opposed to Mozart's minor, owes much to its predecessor in terms of melodiousness and euphonious sounds. Listen with particular care to the two minuets, where stylistic similarities are very apparent.

GROUP 2
A. Beethoven: *Symphony No. 5 (1807)*
B. Beethoven: *Symphony No. 7 (1812)*
1. Brahms: *Symphony No. 1 (1876)*
2. Tchaikovsky: *Symphony No. 4 (1878)*
AB A1 B2 A2

Beethoven's Fifth and Seventh Symphonies, though full of brilliance and drama, distribute their musical weight very differently. The tragedy-to-triumph Fifth is a finale symphony, while the Seventh has its center of gravity in the first movement. Brahms' First, like Beethoven's Fifth, is a finale symphony, though with a different pattern of tension and release. Tchaikovsky's Fourth, like Beethoven's Seventh, tilts the symphonic balance toward the first movement, though Tchaikovsky's is tragic and Beethoven's is jubilant. Also, like the Fifth, the Tchaikovsky presents a victorious struggle against fate. Are the two triumphant finales equally convincing?

The purpose of these comparisons is to acquire a feel for the sequence of moods and emotions that comprises music in several movements. Listen with an ear to discovering how the various parts interact, and where the composer chooses to place the greatest musical emphasis. What do the first-movement introductions to the Beethoven Seventh and the Brahms do for the movements as a whole? Why does Brahms' finale also require an introduction? Does the reappearance of the "Fate" theme in the finale of the Tchaikovsky show the surrounding festivities in a different light?

GROUP 3
A. Copland: *Appalachian Spring (1944)*
B. Britten: *Four Sea Interludes*
from "Peter Grimes" (Chapter 9) (1945)
1. Goldmark: *Rustic Wedding Symphony (1876)*
2. Handel: *Water Music (1717)*
AB A1 B2 A2 12

This is music about the outdoors, or music actually meant to be played there. Copland and Britten share a certain "open air" quality produced by springy rhythms and widely spaced orchestration—high, exposed violins and woodwinds opposite low brass and strings, with not much in the middle. Goldmark's attractive symphony, like *Appalachian Spring,* is about a country wedding, and both composers flavor their themes with folk music.

Handel's *Water Music* was written to be played on a barge in the middle of the river Thames. Note the predominance of wind-based sonorities, which would carry better in an outdoor environment than strings. In fact, the other three works also favor winds and brass whenever the composer wants to create a feeling of being outside, or in the country. Associating music that minimizes or eliminates the participation of string instruments with rustic or open-air settings is practically a universal constant in our musical culture.

GROUP 4
A. Sousa: *Marches (1880–1920)*
B. Elgar: *Pomp and Circumstance (1901–30)*
1. Mahler: *Symphony No. 3 (1896)*
2. Hindemith: *Symphonic Metamorphosis on Themes
by Carl Maria von Weber (1943)*
AB A1 A2 12

Everyone should own a collection of Sousa marches, the greatest works of their kind. But marches are also a feature of our symphonic tradition. Elgar's put on a more formal dress (even a graduation cap and gown), as does the brilliant finale of Hindemith's delightful paraphrase of Weber tunes. Mahler's Third Symphony features, in its first movement, an all-out battle between two marches: one slow and funereal, the other fast and lively. The wild passage in the middle of the movement, with four screaming piccolos, gives the similar moment in Sousa's "Stars and Stripes Forever" a run for its money.

GROUP 5
A. Bach: *Brandenburg Concertos (1720)*
B. Vivaldi: *The Four Seasons (Chapter 3) (1725)*
1. Stravinsky: *Dumbarton Oaks (1938)*
2. Stravinsky: *Pulcinella (1920)*
AB A1 B2 12

If hearing the difference between Haydn and Mozart often proves problematic for the beginner, distinguishing between Baroque composers is even more difficult. The farther from us in time a style is, the less individual its practitioners seem. But differences do exist, especially between the Italian and German schools, as typified by Vivaldi and Bach. For the Italian school, the prime consideration is frequently melodic, with singing tunes and lyrical turns of phrase. The Germans prefer motivic development, with polyphonic mastery an important musical goal. But these distinctions can be hard to hear, particularly when they represent to some extent a nineteenth-century nationalistic viewpoint based on selective historical hindsight. Bach wrote marvelous melodies, and Vivaldi was no contrapuntal slouch.

To put these ideas into perspective, consider the two Stravinsky pieces, both of which exaggerate the salient features of the two different schools. *Pulcinella* (the suite or the complete ballet with songs) is mostly a reworking of music by Italian Baroque composer Giovanni Pergolesi. *Dumbarton Oaks,* similarly based on Bach's Brandenburgs (particularly the Third) provides an easily audible contrast.

GROUP 6

A. Dvořák: *Slavonic Dances (1878–86)*
B. Liszt: *Totentanz (Chapter 6) (1853)*
1. Bartók: *Dance Suite (1923)*
2. Rachmaninoff: *Symphonic Dances (1940)*
AB A1 B2

As we saw in Part One, both the march and the dance have been vastly influential in the evolution of instrumental music. Dvořák's Slavonic Dances acknowledge this debt, being symphonic realizations of actual peasant dance rhythms—though the tunes are original. Liszt's *Totentanz* takes a more abstract view of the dance concept—namely, a study in motion.

Bartók's Dance Suite, like the Dvořák, looks to folk dances for inspiration, but the style has become brasher and less literal. Rachmaninoff's Symphonic Dances turns Liszt's concept into a fullfledged symphony, and even shares in its finale a sinister shadow in the form of the *Dies irae.*

GROUP 7
A. Ravel: *Concerto for the Left Hand (1931)*
B. Gershwin: *Rhapsody in Blue (1924)*
1. Weill: *Suite from "The Threepenny Opera"*
(Kleine Dreigroschenmusik) (1929)
2. Milhaud: *The Creation of the World (1923)*
AB A1 B2

Jazz has had a major influence on many twentieth-century composers. The classic example of this is Gershwin, who nevertheless actually sought lessons from Ravel. The French composer refused, for fear of destroying Gershwin's originality. The immortal *Rhapsody in Blue* employs jazz materials throughout, while Ravel's single-movement concerto features a jazz-inflected central episode. Both Ravel and Weill, embedding jazz elements in a European musical tradition, seem to relate the style to sinister, decadent, and even vulgar moods. Milhaud, writing after the style of Harlem dance bands, like Gershwin has absorbed his influences thoroughly, and does not employ jazz in order to have it intrude into a basically European vocabulary.

GROUP 8
A. Brahms: *Symphony No. 4 (Chapter 5) (1885)*
B. Bruckner: *Symphony No. 4 (rev. 1880)*
1. Dvořák: *Symphony No. 7 (Chapter 7) (1885)*
2. Hindemith: *Nobilissima Visione (1938)*
AB A1 B2 A2

Brahms and Bruckner were the two great German symphonists of the late Romantic era. Although they were very different, these two symphonies show them as close together as they were to come. Brahms, especially in his slow movement, approaches something like the bardic, mythical world of twilight forests echoing with horn calls that Bruckner so magically evokes.

Dvořák's Seventh may very well have influenced Brahms in writing his Fourth, though the two works are roughly contemporaneous. It's a grandly tragic piece, and easily Dvořák's greatest symphony. Compare the two first movements, noting the catastrophic passage in each wherein a huge, major-key climax turns tragically minor.

Hindemith's work is a ballet on the life of St. Francis of Assisi. The finale, like that of Brahms' Fourth, is a passacaglia, but the blocklike, unblended sonorities and archaic-sounding harmonies recall Bruckner. Note especially the similarities between Bruckner and Hindemith in writing for brass and winds, often without the rich cushion of strings so essential to Brahms and Dvořák.

GROUP 9

A. Berlioz: *Symphonie fantastique (Chapter 9) (1830)*
B. Schumann: *Symphony No. 3 ("Rhenish") (1850)*
1. Beethoven: *Symphony No. 6 ("Pastoral") (1808)*
2. Mahler: *Symphony No. 1 (1888)*
AB A1 B2 12

In this group, the concept of "program" music runs smack into the "absolute" conception of the symphony. Berlioz's work is clearly programmatic, and is unified by a theme recurring in all five movements. Schumann's Third is inspired by the German countryside, but lacks specific imagery. Beethoven's Sixth is the conceptual parent of both the Berlioz and the Schumann. It contains both Schumann's pastoralisms, and in its third and fourth movements, some of Berlioz's programmatic specificity. Notice also that all three composers adopt a five-movement form, the music's descriptive aspects providing convenient justification.

Mahler's First began life as a five-movement symphonic poem, but lost its second movement (called "Blumine") and became a symphony. The work clearly shows the influence of Schumann and Beethoven in its overtly rustic orientation. If the opening movement doesn't evoke the gradual awakening of a country morning, then nothing does. Also, compare Mahler's second movement to Schumann's, and to the "Pastoral's" third movement: three representations of peasant dancing. Mahler even quotes the brass chorale with descending string flourishes from the end of Schumann's finale in his own.

GROUP 10

A. Beethoven: *Leonore Overture No. 3 (1806)*
B. Rossini: *Overture to "The Barber of Seville" (1813)*
1. Weber: *Overture to "Der Freischütz" (1820)*
2. Bernstein: *Overture to "Candide" (1956)*
AB A1 B2

Beethoven and Rossini were contemporaries, though Rossini was much the younger. The difference between the two can be neatly summed up by the fact that Beethoven wrote four overtures for his single opera, *Fidelio* (or *Leonore),* while Rossini's *Barber, Aureliano in Palmira,* and *Elizabeth, Queen of England* all used the same overture. Beethoven's, though magnificent alone, is inextricably bound up with *Fidelio,* and so neatly summarizes the subject that he had to detach it, for it rendered the opera itself virtually unnecessary! Rossini's overture, by contrast, would make a great curtain raiser to just about anything.

Weber, in his *Freischütz* Overture, continues in the Beethoven mold, while Bernstein's overture to *Candide* is the nearest thing to Rossini available nowadays.

GROUP II

A. Vaughan Williams: *Symphony No. 6 (1947)*
B. Shostakovich: *Symphony No. 8 (1943)*
1. Honegger: *Symphony No. 3 ("Liturgique") (1946)*
2. Prokofiev: *Symphony No. 6 (1946)*
ALL

Great events often influence artists, but the precise nature of this influence can be hard to pinpoint. In these four works, you can judge for yourself the effect that World War II may have had on their composers. The Vaughan Williams and Shostakovich symphonies both appeared immediately in the wake of optimistic predecessors. The finale of Vaughan Williams' Sixth was said to depict nuclear desolation, though the composer vigorously denied this. Honegger's Third has three movements that take titles from the Requiem Mass for the Dead. Compare the motor rhythms of its opening movement to the beginning of the Vaughan Williams, and the third movement of the Shostakovich.

In the Soviet Union under Stalin, World War II ironically provided a brief taste of artistic freedom. The vast and tragic loss of human life allowed composers to ignore the optimistic party line and create elegies dedicated to "the victims of fascism." Both Prokofiev and Shostakovich do precisely this, though Prokofiev's symphony ends in brazen defiance while his compatriot's collapses into a state of numb, semitranquil exhaustion (as do the Honegger and Vaughan Williams). All four works employ march rhythms and contrast these with more lyrical, affirmative elements that get roundly pulverized by the mindless mechanism of war.

GROUP 12

A. Wagner: *Venusberg Music from "Tannhäuser"* (Chapter 9) (1860)
B. Saint-Saëns: *Bacchanale from "Samson and Delilah"* (Chapter 9) (1877)
1. Verdi: *Aida* (1870)
2. Ravel: *Ma Mère l'Oye (Mother Goose) (complete)* (1912)
AB A1 B2

Composers, especially those of opera, have always been attracted by the opportunity to explore exotic settings and thus enlarge their musical palette. Wagner's *Tannhäuser* ballet, which opens the opera immediately following the overture in the Paris version, is a delightfully inept example of musical exoticism. Not only does the rabidly nationalist Wagner move Venus to Germany, but he makes her a castanet player as well! Saint-Saëns, by contrast, gets it right in his literally Philistine "Bacchanale."

Verdi was Wagner's great Italian contemporary, and his *Aida* is one of the most popular operas ever written. Get the whole work, sit down with the text, and listen to Verdi's colorful and dramatic evocation of ancient Egypt. Both the Verdi and the Wagner owe a debt to French grand opera, which demanded a ballet, great spectacle, and magnificent choruses in every work. These were the origins of those Hollywood extravaganzas employing a "cast of thousands."

Ravel's *Mother Goose* ballet (do not get the suite) explores the exotic world of fairy tales in one of the most beautiful and enchanting pieces of orchestration ever devised. All four composers emphasize "exotic" instruments such as harps, flutes and, above all, percussion. This was never Wagner's strong suit, hence his hilarious castanets. Verdi achieves much with flutes and triangle, while the French have always reveled in the orchestral opportunities offered by exotic subject matter.

GROUP 13
A. de Falla: *The Three-Cornered Hat (complete) (1919)*
B. Schreker: *Chamber Symphony (1917)*
1. Stravinsky: *Pétrouchka (1911)*
2. Schoenberg: *Chamber Symphony No. 1 (1906)*
AB A1 A2 12

Manuel de Falla and Franz Schreker have little in common save a great love of making beautiful sounds. They represent the mellowing process that often occurs after certain absolutist positions have been set forth. Specifically, Stravinsky and Schoenberg in this example (but not as a rule) can be seen as polar opposites. Schoenberg's Chamber Symphony compresses the maximum amount of development into the most compact possible form, and the restricted instrumental color focuses the attention on thematic and motivic activities. Stravinsky's popular ballet isn't developmental at all, but exists solely as a celebration of instrumental virtuosity based on material not only repetitious, but frequently trivial. For Stravinsky, the surface *is* the music, while Schoenberg's intricacies require repeated and sympathetic listening.

Schreker's Chamber Symphony, though clearly based on Schoenberg's model, is as hedonistically lovely as Schoenberg's is austerely difficult. It's full of purely coloristic passages for instruments like the celesta, with its tinkling bell sounds. De Falla's Spanish folk ballet, despite the conceptual debt to the Stravinsky, employs material of far greater thematic distinction in a more highly developed manner. Music is seldom philosophically consistent, and the first or most extreme example of any artistic tendency may not necessarily be the best.

GROUP 14
A. Bach: *Orchestral Suites (Overtures) (1720)*
B. Zelenka: *Capriccios (1723)*
1. Schoenberg: *Suite for Strings in G (1934)*
2. Enescu (or Enesco): *Orchestral Suites (1903–38)*
AB A1 B2 12

The Baroque orchestral suite, discussed in Chapter 3, never completely disappeared. It experienced an especially strong resurgence in modern times. Bach's four Overtures and Jan Zelenka's five Capriccios (another name for the same thing) show this tradition at its original, Baroque best. Zelenka, in particular, is a tremendously unappreciated composer who combines contrapuntal ingenuity with great harmonic daring, possibly influenced by the folk music of his native Czechoslovakia.

Schoenberg's Suite pays affectionate tribute to the world of Bach. Despite this composer's notorious reputation as the man who destroyed tonality, this elegant exercise in neoclassicism holds no terrors for even the casual listener. Like Zelenka, Enesco combined the overture concept with folk inflections; though as befits a twentieth-century nationalist, the ethnic influence is much stronger. Enesco wrote three suites for orchestra, all of which are worthwhile. For starters, listen to the wonderful prelude for unison strings that begins the First Suite, or try the delightful Bourrée that concludes the Second.

GROUP 15

A. Janáček: *Sinfonietta (Chapter 10) (1926)*
B. Roussel: *Symphony No. 3 (1930)*
1. Bruckner: *Symphony No. 8 (1890)*
2. Copland: *Short Symphony (1933)*
AB A1 B2

This group has been assembled with an ear toward hearing different types of rhythmic motion. Both Janáček and Roussel employ forceful, driving rhythms to propel their music forward. The Sinfonietta, for twelve trumpets with orchestra, uses a technique called *ostinato,* which refers to an "obstinate" repetition of rhythmic patterns. Roussel prefers strongly accented triple or duple rhythms.

Bruckner shares something of Janáček's rhythmic and thematic technique. Like the Czech composer, his music frequently consists of a mosaic of short themes that build up through repetition into larger structures. But whereas Janáček's rhythmic pace is very quick, Bruckner's is exceptionally slow. Just one of these mosaic structures serves Janáček for an entire movement, while Bruckner's movements often consist of the contrasts between several. Compare, for example, the Sinfonietta's fourth movement with the Eighth's scherzo (second movement), listening to the steady repetition of brief melodies in both cases. Bruckner's single movement is two thirds as long as the Sinfonietta, and his slow movement and finale are each longer than the entire work.

Copland, like Roussel, drives his music with great rhythmic zest. But he prefers syncopated rhythms: that is, with unexpected accents placed off the beat. Roussel employs this effect very wittily in the third movement of his symphony, where the cymbals try to trip up the rest of the orchestra. With Copland, syncopation is a stylistic feature throughout.

GROUP 16
A. Mahler: *Symphony No. 6 (1904)*
B. Sibelius: *Symphony No. 4 (1911)*
1. Berg: *Three Pieces for Orchestra (1915)*
2. Walton: *Symphony No. 1 (1935)*
AB A1 B2

Mahler's Sixth and Sibelius's Fourth illustrate the difference between genuine tragedy and bleak desolation. The Mahler is tragic, and like all tragedies represents a struggle against fate, symbolized by a recurring drum rhythm over which a bright major chord turns ominously minor. Unlike Brahms' Fourth (see Chapter 5), the tragic catastrophes occur in the last movement, at the two hammer blows. Fate triumphs as each theme proves to be derived from its two symbols: the rhythm and the changing chord. Sibelius's Fourth is his most impersonal symphony. In terms of thematic materials, it's closely related to *Tapiola* (see Chapter 10). The brief moments of human lyricism that exist flicker out against an impassive and dark landscape.

Berg's Three Pieces take the language of Mahler's Sixth, sledgehammers and all, and carry it into the world of atonality. The music is difficult, but ultimately very beautiful, and the nightmarish concluding march is a "Friday the Thirteenth"–style gutwrencher. Walton's First takes Sibelius's musical vocabulary and forces it into a Beethovenian, tragedy-to-triumph progression. Compare the way in which long, swelling melodies over rapid string ostinatos (see Group 15) create an impression of athletic movement.

Start with the Mahler, but give all four works a chance when you feel ready. The moods expressed are more difficult than the styles conveying them.

GROUP 17
A. Johann Strauss, Jr.: *Waltzes (1865–90)*
B. Saint-Saëns: *Danse Macabre (1874)*
1. Richard Strauss: *Also Sprach Zarathustra (Chapter 9)*
(1896)
2. Ravel: *La Valse (1920)*
ALL

Waltzes have long been popular with great composers, from the Waltz King, Johann Strauss, Jr., himself, to the present. Each of the Strauss waltzes is actually a suite of dances arranged in a symmetrical pattern. Saint-Saëns' little tone poem is a sarcastic waltz parody, popularized in several Halloween cartoons in which skeletons play the xylophone on their rib cages.

Richard Strauss' (no relation) tone poem after Nietzsche is the one that Kubrick used in *2001: A Space Odyssey.* It has a terrific waltz in its second half. What? You've never heard the second half? Ravel's waltz, like Saint-Saëns', takes a distorted view of the dance, as Vienna whirls itself into a holocaust of violence. Its structure closely resembles Strauss'.

GROUP 18
A. Dvořák: *Symphony No. 9*
("From the New World") (1893)
B. Debussy: *Nocturnes (1899)*
1. Vaughan Williams: *A London Symphony (1920)*
2. de Falla: *Nights in the Gardens of Spain (1915)*
AB A1 B2 12

Vast tracts of nonsense have been written about Dvořák's debt to Negro spirituals and American music, but the title says it all.

The symphony was written from, not about, the New World, and it expresses the composer's longing for his homeland. The music is as Czech as his Slavonic Dances (see Group 6). Debussy's Nocturnes are music as nationalistically oriented as Dvořák's, but not in any melodic sense.

In every country but France and Germany, musical nationalism involved the incorporation of ethnic and folk melodic elements into the basic Germanic orchestral style. But France and Germany had too old and established a musical culture to pursue this course. After the Wagner/Brahms/Bruckner apotheosis, German music faced a regenerative crisis from which it never recovered, and musical hegemony passed elsewhere, especially to France. The French, with their openness to outside cultural influences, evolved several styles more easily classifiable according to subject than musical technique. Virtually all major French music written in the past hundred years takes as its inspirational source classical Greece, Spain, the Orient, or the French Baroque.

Although technically "impressionist" music, of the three Nocturnes "Fêtes" is Spanish, and "Sirènes" hails from the seas of Greek myth. De Falla's work is a Spanish nocturne by a Spanish composer —compare with Debussy. Vaughan Williams' gorgeous symphony does for England what Dvořák's does for Czechoslovakia—not without a glance at Debussy's and de Falla's sound world.

GROUP 19

A. Mozart: *Symphony No. 41 ("Jupiter")* (1788)
B. Haydn: *Symphony No. 104 ("London")* (1795)
1. Handel: *Royal Fireworks Music* (1749)
2. Beethoven: *Symphony No. 2* (1802)
AB A1 B1 B2 12

None of these works requires a large orchestra, but all of them have a magisterial grandeur about them for which the only adequate word is "pomp." Mozart's 41st Symphony features a contrapuntal finale that still amazes in its resource and majesty. Haydn's last symphony opens with a flourish of trumpets and drums that strikes a note of profound solemnity. Compare the similar introduction to Beethoven's first movement.

All three of these composers admired Handel immensely. Beethoven thought him the greatest "ancient" master; Mozart arranged a new version of *Messiah;* and Haydn wrote his late oratorios *The Creation* and *The Seasons* under the musical influence of England's Handel festivals. Perhaps all three of these composers show, though we have nothing concrete to prove it, that they could express something of Handel's extraordinary breadth and vigor in terms of the Classical symphony. Listen to the Fireworks Music, and see if you don't agree.

GROUP 20

A. Beethoven: *Symphony No. 9 ("Choral") (1824)*
B. Schubert: *Symphony No. 9 ("The Great") (1828)*
1. Mahler: *Symphony No. 2 ("Resurrection") (1894)*
2. Haydn: *Symphony No. 103 ("Drumroll") (1795)*
AB A1 B2 12

Beethoven was the last composer of the Classical period, Schubert among the first of the Romantic. Their careers overlap almost exactly, owing to Schubert's early death at age thirty-one, and here they meet on common symphonic ground. In his Ninth, Beethoven bursts through Classical convention and adds a choral finale to his design. Schubert, the greatest songwriter in history, disciplines his lyrical gift and writes a grand, but thoroughly Classical symphony. The famous "Ode to Joy" theme from Beethoven's Ninth makes a brief appearance in Schubert's finale. Coincidence or design?

Mahler's "Resurrection" Symphony takes the first movement and finale of the Beethoven as obvious models, but otherwise differs dramatically. Haydn's "Drumroll" Symphony, aside from an opening reference to the *Dies irae,* which it shares with the Mahler, has a second movement that is a distant ancestor of Schubert's. Both feature themes that are minor-key marches with similar rhythmic figures. But as with Mahler and Beethoven, the differences are just as great. You will enjoy discovering them for yourself.

GROUP 21

A. Hindemith: *"Mathis der Maler" Symphony (1934)*
B. Shostakovich: *Symphony No. 5 (1937)*
1. Ives: *Symphony No. 4 (1916)*
2. Berio: *Sinfonia (1968)*
AB A1 B2 12

These four compositions represent different solutions to the problem of finding an audience for modern music. Hindemith's symphony affirmed his desire to write music at once approachable and challenging. Ironically, this attractive work, which begins with a "Concert of Angels" and incorporates Lutheran church chorales, became a focal point in the struggle for artistic freedom against Nazi policies. Shostakovich wrote his Fifth after having been severely criticized by the Communist party for composing antisocialist music. Though more approachable than his earlier works in the form, does the finale, after the ghostly slow movement, actually represent a triumph, or is it merely bombastic and shallow?

If Hindemith and Shostakovich were conciliatory toward their audiences, then Ives and Berio were confrontational. Ives, like Hindemith, created a new music out of his rich musical heritage, but he did so without much concern for listenability. Nevertheless, the Fourth Symphony is a masterpiece containing a second-movement collage based on American popular tunes, and a finale of truly mysterious beauty. Listen with a sense of humor, and you'll have fun with it. Berio's *Sinfonia*, though not written under party pressure, is the most political document of the four works. It combines an Ivesian collage based on our Western musical tradition (starting with the scherzo of Mahler's Second Symphony) with a whispered tribute to Martin Luther King, Jr. Eight singers contribute to the fracas by chanting, singing, and speaking several different texts in various languages. As an attempt to introduce a 1960s form of political and social consciousness into a thorny musical idiom, *Sinfonia* is a unique and fascinating success.

GROUP 22

A. Brahms: *Symphony No. 2 (1878)*

B. Wagner: *Prelude and Liebestod from "Tristan und Isolde" (1865)*

1. Dvořák: *Symphony No. 6 (1880)*

2. Schoenberg: *Verklärte Nacht (Transfigured Night) (1899)*

AB A1 B2

Here, in a nutshell, is one of the great musical controversies of the nineteenth century. Brahms and Wagner were both hailed as Beethoven's heir: Brahms for his revitalization of the Classical symphony, and Wagner for his application of symphonic techniques to opera. Listen to each representative piece, noting the very marked differences in style.

Dvořák's Sixth owes a debt to Brahms' Second, especially if you compare the two finales. Similarly, Schoenberg's lovely piece (for string sextet or string orchestra, either version is fine) remains one of his most popular and appealing. It expands on the language of Wagner's *Tristan,* in which chromaticism is very important. This means that both composers frequently employ musical phrases and harmonies containing notes that are foreign to, or that "color" (Greek: *chroma),* the basic key. The effect obscures tonality, producing a sense of restless, timeless yearning as expected resolutions avoid fulfilling our tonal expectations. Though perfectly acceptable to the ear now, this style shocked contemporary audiences, and was indeed the first step on the path to complete atonality.

GROUP 2 3
A. Poulenc: *Concert Champêtre*
for Harpsichord and Orchestra (1928)
B. Ravel: *Piano Concerto in G (1931)*
1. Bach: *Harpsichord Concerto in D minor (1730)*
2. Mozart: *Piano Concerto No. 21 (1785)*
AB A1 B2

Both Poulenc and Ravel were modern French composers who produced keyboard concertos in imitation of Baroque and Classical models. Though he shares the use of the harpsichord with Bach, Poulenc is marvelously eclectic, shamelessly juxtaposing Baroque melodic clichés with Parisian street music and rustic bugle calls. The opening of the finale sounds the most Bach-like. Ravel's concerto, with its jazz overtones, tries to embody the elegance and simplicity of the Mozart (compare the slow movements) while ignoring the questions of form that the earlier composer solved so successfully.

GROUP 2 4
A. Nielsen: *Symphony No. 4 ("The Inextinguishable")*
(1916)
B. Sibelius: *Symphony No. 5 (1918)*
1. Schumann: *Symphony No. 4 (1841)*
2. Mozart: *Symphony No. 38 ("Prague") (1786)*
AB A1 B2

Here are two classic Scandinavian symphonies (see Group 30), each deviating slightly from the standard form, and each paired with a similarly structured German symphony. Nielsen's Fourth runs all four movements together, though they remain structurally distinct. The first and last movements are united by a recurring, triumphant theme. Sibelius's Fifth takes only three movements, as does Mozart's "Prague" Symphony. Notice how both composers, despite stylistic differences, write first movements that include lengthy slow introductions (in Sibelius's case amounting to half the movement), creating a quasi–four movement, slow-fast-slow-fast structure.

Like Nielsen in his Fourth, Schumann directed that all four movements be played without a break. Also, both symphonies move from minor-key beginnings to major-key conclusions. To what extent do you think that musical continuity affects this overall progression?

GROUP 25
A. Wagner: *Orchestral Excerpts from Der Ring des Nibelungen* (*1876*)
B. Wagner: *Rienzi Overture* (*1840*)
1. Scriabin: *Symphony No. 2* (*1901*)
2. Rossini: *Overture to "The Thieving Magpie"* (*1817*)
AB A1 B2

It's impossible to overestimate Wagner's influence on musical scholarship—which is not the same thing as on music. For an entirely too complex series of social, political, cultural, philosophical, and methodological reasons, Wagner has become a convenient landmark. Nothing escaped his influence. Aside from its intellectual convenience, this view is nonsense. Granted, Wagner's music appealed to many, and comparison between the music from the *Ring* (which includes the "Ride of the Valkyries" of *Apocalypse Now* fame) and Scriabin's Second Symphony shows Wagner's influence very clearly.

On the other hand, Wagner didn't come from a vacuum. He was influenced even as he affected others. Comparison of the early

Rienzi Overture with the Rossini reveals Wagner as a sluggish Italian with no sense of humor. Wagner's real achievement lies in the distance traveled from this early work to the supreme musical mastery of the *Ring, Tristan,* and *Die Meistersinger.* That you can hear for yourself, without worrying about any cultural generalizations.

GROUP 26
A. Dvořák: *Symphony No. 8 (1889)*
B. Smetana: *Má Vlast (My Country) (1879)*
1. Suk: *A Summer Tale (1908)*
2. Janáček: *Taras Bulba (1918)*
ALL

The musical culture of Czechoslovakia is still underappreciated in the West. This country's musical pedigree is as rich, continuous, and distinguished as France's or Germany's, and a lot less pretentious than either. Smetana was the first great Czech nationalist composer, and his cycle of six tone poems glorifying his homeland was a true labor of love. His tragic deafness made it certain that he would never hear the work. The second in the set, "Vltava" (The Moldau), has achieved great popularity independently.

Dvořák took Smetana's achievement into the world of "absolute" music in his nine symphonies, of which the Eighth is the least traditional in both form and content. It thrives on colorful orchestration and Czech melody rather than thematic development, despite a standard four-movement format. Josef Suk was Dvořák's son-in-law. *A Summer Tale* is the second in a tetralogy of magnificent works that brought Czech music into the twentieth century. The third movement, "Blind Fiddlers," with its two English horns and harp, attains a rare degree of eloquence and poetry.

Janáček, probably *the* great opera composer of this century, enlarged the field of Czech musical inspiration to include other Slavic peoples. *Taras Bulba,* a glorious "rhapsody for orchestra," sets a Russian legend. All four composers share a rhythmic vitality, songfulness, and orchestral brilliance (woodwinds to the fore) that is typically Czech.

GROUP 27
A. Mahler: *Symphony No. 5 (1902)*
B. Delius: *Sea Drift (1903)*
1. Haydn: *Symphony No. 100 ("Military") (1795)*
2. Vaughan Williams: *A Sea Symphony (1909)*
AB A1 B2

Not all Romantic composers were nationalists. Mahler and Delius represent the cosmopolitan side of European music. As a German Jew born in Bohemia, Mahler's style is profoundly inclusive. The Fifth, which is typical of his aesthetic, has a bit of everything: a sleazy funeral march, a complex sonata-form second movement, a wild waltz of a scherzo, a heartfelt song for strings and harp, and a virtuosic fugal finale.

Delius, British born, educated in Germany, and a citizen of France, evolved a hermetic style noteworthy for its lack of eclecticism. His music is unusually quiet, meditative, frequently almost rhythmless, and rapturously nature-intoxicated. *Sea Drift* sets a Walt Whitman text, and is an exact contemporary of Mahler's Fifth. Whitman's poetry was a powerful stimulus to English composers at the turn of the century. Vaughan Williams' symphony, composed to a Whitman text a few years after *Sea Drift,* makes for a uniquely logical comparison.

Haydn, like Mahler, was happy to integrate the widest range of influences into his symphonic style. Both the "Military" Symphony and the Fifth incorporate the same Austrian military trumpet call into their respective march movements, and feature (in Haydn for the first time ever in a symphony) the new standard "military" percussion of bass drum with cymbals, though Mahler's march is as ghostly as Haydn's is ebullient. Also, both composers were among the greatest masters of orchestration. Every instrument, from timpani on up, receives a rewarding and idiomatic solo; and the musical lines always move with unobtrusive clarity.

GROUP 28
A. Hindemith: *Symphony in E-flat (1940)*
B. Stravinsky: *Symphony in Three Movements (1945)*
1. Kokkonen: *Symphony No. 4 (1971)*
2. Martin: *Petite Symphonie Concertante (1945)*
AB A1 B2 12 A2

Hindemith and Stravinsky seldom wrote symphonies, but the ones they did write number among their finest works. Hindemith's has a strong military streak: a heroic first movement prefaces a nobly elegiac funeral march. The scherzo is skittish and mercurial, with a pastoral trio, while the finale is a dogged march that fights through to a triumphant conclusion.

Stravinsky's symphony is a "concertante" work—a cross between a symphony and a concerto. The first movement features a piano, the second a harp, and the finale combines the two. Like the Hindemith, the piece projects a certain militant aggressiveness, as does Swiss composer Frank Martin's marvelous piece for harp, harpsichord, piano, and string orchestra. In two movements, the second features a march tune uncannily similar to that in the first movement of Joonas Kokkonen's Fourth, which in turn harks back to the finale of the Hindemith symphony.

Kokkonen, one of the greatest living Finnish composers, evolves his themes out of a musical fog from which melodic fragments gradually fit together to form a complete tune. His second-movement scherzo, with its flickering swiftness and percussive rattling, curiously recalls Hindemith's. Once again we find that similar ideas receive similar treatment, however different basic styles may be.

GROUP 29

A. Beethoven: *Piano Concerto No. 5 ("Emperor") (1809)*
B. Weber: *Konzertstück in F minor (1821)*
1. Brahms: *Piano Concerto No. 1 (1858)*
2. Schumann: *Piano Concerto (1845)*
ALL

This group merely introduces some pieces not touched upon (Weber aside) in Chapter 7. The Beethoven and Brahms are "justification" concertos, while the Weber and Schumann are "virtuoso" works. If you worked through "Solo Personalities," then these concertos should pose no problems at all.

GROUP 30

A. Nielsen: *Symphony No. 3 ("Espansiva") (1911)*
B. Stenhammar: *Symphony No. 2 (1915)*
1. Tubin: *Symphony No. 2 ("Legendary") (1938)*
2. Sibelius: *Symphony No. 7 (1926)*
ALL

Scandinavian composers in the early decades of this century had a certain conservative streak. Their music stayed resolutely tonal, and often featured (like the Czechs') an invigorating rhythmic profile combined with folk-influenced melodies. Nielsen, a Dane and one of the truly great symphonists, wrote in a style noteworthy for its tremendous vitality, as well as its humanity and warmth.

Wilhelm Stenhammar, from Sweden, became increasingly classically oriented as he matured, and produced in his Second Symphony a sparkling work full of lucid contrapuntal textures. Eduard Tubin's "Legendary" Symphony lives up to its name, being more obviously colorful and Romantic than the other works here, even though it came later. Although he settled in Sweden, Tubin was Estonian, and something of Russian passion and melancholy certainly affected his basically Nordic orientation.

Sibelius is for many the quintessential Scandinavian composer. His Seventh (and last) Symphony, in one movement, neatly sums up the austerity, grandeur, pastoral charm, and occasional mystery characteristic of all four composers. What Sibelius lacked, and what Nielsen had in abundance, was a flair for the vocally inspired melody that defines human emotion. Listen to Nielsen's second movement: when the two wordless voices enter, the impersonal music that preceded them becomes a background to a populated landscape. Sibelius's musical terrain remains resolutely unpeopled.

GROUP 31
A. Mahler. *Das Lied von der Erde*
(The Song of the Earth) (1909)
B. Ravel: *Schéhérazade (song cycle) (1903)*
1. Zemlinsky: *Lyric Symphony (1922)*
2. Dukas: *La Péri (1912)*
AB A1 B2

The Orient has always been a source of inspiration to Western composers, though the German and French schools express this very differently. Mahler responded first to the meaning of the text, sensing kinship in Chinese poetry's fatalistic longing, nostalgia, and bittersweet loneliness. Although passages do sound "Chinese," the philosophy is more important. The same can be said of Zemlinsky's work, which he admittedly based on *Das Lied.* Both are multimovement song-symphonies for large orchestra with alternating male and female soloists, based on Oriental poetry.

Ravel and Dukas use the Orient as an excuse to create the sensuous sounds they so adore, as well as to write instrumental music that is specifically non-Germanic, formally speaking. Ravel's song cycle is, at first, a travelogue, and then a series of erotically voluptuous images. Whereas Mahler and Zemlinsky naturally reveal their Orientalism in terms of the symphony, Dukas's ballet creates a successful structure as far from sonata form as Berlin is from its Persian setting. Germans opt for truth, the French for beauty. But as Keats said, "Beauty is truth, truth beauty," and each method achieves its own success.

GROUP 32

A. Vaughan Williams: *Symphony No. 3 ("Pastoral") (1921)*
B. Elgar: *Symphony No. 2 (1911)*
1. Moeran: *Symphony in G minor (1937)*
2. Bax: *Symphony No. 2 (1926)*
ALL

The sources of inspiration for the English symphony have been more various than in most other countries, perhaps owing to England's position as a great mercantile and cultural crossroad—not to mention a lapsed domestic musical tradition, virtually inert since the Baroque, that encouraged composers to seek inspiration abroad. Vaughan Williams studied in France with Ravel, and his Third Symphony shows a decidedly French predilection for shimmering, sensuous sound. Even more obvious is the composer's deep love of English Renaissance music, and folksong (see Group 37).

Elgar despised folksong, and created in his music an amalgam of the styles of Brahms and Richard Strauss. He gets the best of both worlds in his Second Symphony, placing Strauss's orchestral opulence (see Group 39) in the service of real thematic and motivic development. Bax, by contrast, conceals his formal processes under a dense layer of instrumental luxuriance. His aesthetic, based on his love of an imaginary Celtic past, owes much to the exoticism of Ravel (see Group 12), and can make even Elgar seem austere.

E. J. Moeran, like Vaughan Williams, writes out of the English folk tradition—known today as the "Pastoral School." To this style he brings a complete identification with the working methods of Sibelius (see Group 16). Notice the sense of forward drive he imparts to his music, and pay special attention to his Sibelian use of string ostinatos (repeated rhythmic patterns).

GROUP 33
A. Respighi: *Roman Trilogy (Chapter 9) (1917–29)*
B. Holst: *The Planets (Chapter 9) (1916)*
1. Grofé: *Grand Canyon Suite (1931)*
2. Mussorgsky/Ravel: *Pictures at an Exhibition (1874)*
ALL

All four of these composers were famous for their stunning writing for instruments. Respighi's set of symphonic poems, *The Pines of Rome, The Fountains of Rome,* and *Roman Festivals,* make a trilogy in homage to both the Eternal City and the modern orchestra. Holst's suite contains not only the original, classic "space" music, it's equally extraordinary in its fascinating treatment of rhythm. (Mars and Neptune are both written in neither duple nor triple meter, but in a genuine rhythm of five.)

Like Respighi, Grofé places his music in the service of scenic description. Mussorgsky, in common with both Holst and Grofé, writes a suite of movements arranged with an ear toward effective musical contrast. Ravel transcribed the piano original for orchestra (as indeed he did most of his own works).

But ask yourself when listening: What are the limits of musical description? Had Respighi written *The Maples of Rome,* could you tell the difference? The subject inspires moods and feelings in the composer, and these he conveys to you. Of course, music can be quite specifically descriptive. Just look at Grofé's "On the Trail." That's surely no maple!

GROUP 34
A. Schoenberg: *Pierrot Lunaire (1912)*
B. Rachmaninoff: *The Isle of the Dead (1909)*
1. Walton: *Façade (complete) (1922)*
2. Tchaikovsky: *Francesca da Rimini (Chapter 7) (1876)*
AB A1 B2

Perhaps at no point in musical history will the disparity in musical styles ever have been greater than in the first decades of this century. The Rachmaninoff and Schoenberg works are about as far apart as it's possible to be while remaining on the same planet. And yet, both composers are expressing virtually the same thing: a nocturnal, morbid atmosphere of seething decadence. *The Isle of the Dead,* based, of course, on the *Dies irae,* is a lusciously Romantic tone poem inspired by Arnold Böcklin's famous painting (usually reproduced on the album cover). *Pierrot Lunaire* is one of the strangest things ever written: a bizarre collection of atonal cabaret songs for voice and chamber ensemble, in which the singer is instructed to speak at pitch rather than produce definite notes. If you're up to it at all, be sure to follow the texts.

Walton's *Façade,* also for speaker and chamber group, is as lighthearted and wacky (and thoroughly tonal) as the Schoenberg is disturbing. There's a delightful orchestral suite, too. Tchaikovsky's Francesca, captive of hell, mournfully pouring out her tale of doomed love, quite possibly inspired Rachmaninoff. Nobody does gloom as well as the Russians.

GROUP 35
A. Brahms: *Symphony No. 3 (1884)*
B. Bruckner: *Symphony No. 9 (1890–96)*
1. Haydn: *Symphony No. 45 ("Farewell") (1772)*
2. Schubert: *Symphony No. 8 ("Unfinished") (1822)*
AB A1 B2

All four of these symphonies end quietly, two of them unintentionally. Group 8 showed Bruckner and Brahms at their most similar. Here, they are poles apart. Brahms' Third is a model of Classical poise and thematic workmanship. Bruckner's last, unfinished symphony explores the composer's technique of opposing monolithic blocks of sound in a way that brings the music into the twentieth century, foreshadowing the "space" music of Holst and Vaughan Williams (see Chapter 9).

Haydn's touching "Farewell" Symphony has a finale that starts Presto, but yields to a slow coda in which the players leave one by one, until only two violins are left. Compare this charming about-face with Brahms' peaceful coda, expressing autumnal tranquillity in the wake of the preceding storm.

Like Bruckner in his Ninth, Schubert got only as far as his slow movement, though in this case the result was a two-movement piece instead of Bruckner's three. Critics and listeners have been virtually unanimous in finding both works perfectly fine as they stand. Do you agree? If so, how do you think this opinion depends on the calm endings of both works? What if Bruckner had placed his scherzo third rather than second?

GROUP 36
A. Mahler: *Symphony No. 7 (1905)*
B. Stravinsky: *The Firebird (suite) (1910)*
1. Bartók: *Concerto for Orchestra (1945)*
2. Messaien: *Turangalîla-symphonie (1948)*
ALL

Here's an interesting correspondence: four works all making musical reference to nocturnal birdsong. Listen to the stylized bird-calls that open the first of the two "Night Music" movements in Mahler's Seventh, and compare the similar imagery in Stravinsky's Introduction and "Dance of the Firebird." Bartók was a master of "night music," as shown in the slow third movement of his Concerto for Orchestra. Like the Mahler, the Bartók has a five-movement "arch" structure, in which a creepy central movement (in Mahler's case a scherzo) is framed by two contrasting character pieces, which are in turn bracketed by fully symphonic first movements and finales. Note also that both works begin with mysterious, nocturnal introductions, and progress to festive celebrations of light.

Messaien's freaky "Turangalîla-symphonie" is one of the wildest and most exciting of all contemporary symphonic works. It alternates schmaltzy tunes that sound like thirties Hollywood film scores with passages of polytonal, rhythmic frenzy that make the "Infernal Danse" in *The Firebird* sound positively anesthetized. Try "The Joy of the Blood of the Stars" for starters. The movement entitled "The Garden of Love's Sleep" evokes the haunting image of birdsong (on piano, glockenspiel, and celesta) over a seemingly end-less hymn to love.

GROUP 37
A. Sibelius: *Symphony No. 6 (1923)*
B. Vaughan Williams: *Fantasia on a Theme*
by Thomas Tallis (1910)
1. Palestrina: *Pope Marcellus Mass (1567)*
2. Tallis: *Spem in alium (Chapter 10) (ca. 1570)*
AB A1 B2 12

Both Sibelius and Vaughan Williams were intrigued by the polyphony of the sixteenth-century masters. Compare the string opening of Sibelius's Sixth to the Vaughan Williams and the Palestrina. Tallis's motet is not the source of Vaughan Williams' tune, but it comes closest to the Fantasia in richness and density of sound.

All four of these works employ modal harmony. Before we had keys there were *modes*. Imagine a piano with no black keys. The scale between two identical notes an octave apart defines a mode. Because there are no black keys to equalize the distance between notes, each modal scale has a slightly different character, often mixing aspects of our major and minor tonalities. Genuine folksong (think of "Greensleeves") is modal, and such music has a curiously haunting, archaic, and timeless quality.

The extraordinary beauty of Renaissance vocal music is hardly known today. The sacred texts of the Mass were, for these composers, analogous to the sonata forms of Classical musicians, and in no way inhibited the most varied musical expression. If it appeals to you, feel free to explore further on your own.

GROUP 38
A. Debussy: *Ibéria (1909)*
B. Ravel: *Rhapsodie Espagnol (1907)*
1. Bizet: *Carmen (suite) (1875)*
2. Rimsky-Korsakov: *Capriccio Espagnol (1887)*
ALL

Spain has been a source of musical inspiration to many composers, and some of the best Spanish music has been written by non-Spaniards, as in this case. Debussy and Ravel were the two leading French composers in the first decades of this century. Compare their respective evocations of Spain. Which of the two sounds more "impressionist" to you? (Personally, Ravel gets my vote.)

Bizet's *Carmen* is perhaps the classic evocation of Spain, and was surely a stimulus to Debussy and Ravel in the sparkling brilliance of its orchestration. Rimsky-Korsakov's lively showpiece highlights the interrelationships that characterize the Russian and French schools. Many French composers, Debussy and Ravel among them, owe their love of coloristic effects to the vivid yet economically scored works of Rimsky-Korsakov and his compatriots (Mussorgsky, Borodin, Balakirev, and Tchaikovsky). Both groups of composers sought to create music in large forms that owed little to Germanic models, and they developed the art of orchestration to a high degree as one aspect of musical technique relatively unexploited by the Germans. Ravel's totally apt setting of Mussorgsky's *Pictures at an Exhibition* (Group 33) is another characteristic example of this fruitful musical liaison.

GROUP 39
A. Strauss: *Don Juan (1888)*
B. Elgar: *In the South (1903)*
1. Bax: *Tintagel (Chapter 9) (1919)*
2. Hanson: *Romantic Symphony (1930)*
AB A1 B2 12

Because of the Germanic bias of musical scholars, Richard Strauss has assumed the role of a sort of post-Wagnerian Wagner. Virtually all music glitzily scored for large orchestra with prominent harps and luscious violins gets laid at his doorstep. Here's a chance to judge for yourself.

Elgar's overture undoubtedly opens like *Don Juan*, but then pursues its own path. Though Elgar learned a few tricks from Strauss, his music is more rugged, less busy, and a bit less impulsive. Bax's glorious seascape owes virtually nothing to Strauss, though it surely equals him in the overwhelming richness of its scoring.

American composers, perhaps because virtually all of the most famous ones studied in France, never developed the sort of opulent, Straussian (for want of a better word) style typical of so many Europeans. Hanson may be about as close as we got. The music of his Romantic Symphony formed part of the sound track to the film *Alien.* Although like Elgar a fine symphonist, Hanson also shares with Bax a love of Celtic legend. You can hear it in the symphony.

In all four examples, try to get past the sheer sound and listen to the way each composer treats his themes. This is the real way to test musical derivation.

GROUP 40
A. Mahler: *Symphony No. 8 (1906)*
B. Schoenberg: *Gurrelieder (1901–11)*
1. Berlioz: *The Damnation of Faust (1854)*
2. Brian: *Gothic Symphony (1927)*
ALL

Here are four of the biggest pieces ever written, using large orchestras, soloists, chorus, extra brass, organs, mandolins, chains, birdcalls, children's choirs—you name it. Paradoxically, it's more important to listen to the subtle colors achieved rather than the huge washes of sound. These tend to take care of themselves, and, considering the forces employed, are relatively few and far between.

Mahler and Berlioz set Goethe's *Faust,* but Berlioz favors the more conventionally picturesque and operatic first part, whereas Mahler busies himself with the mystical and philosophical musings of the second part's final scene: the difference between German and French aesthetics once again? Schoenberg's gorgeous and very Romantic monsterpiece sets a gothic horror story of love, treachery, and doom.

Havergal Brian's gigantic work is probably the largest symphony ever written that gets played from time to time. In his ninety-six-year life span, Brian composed thirty-two symphonies, and he remains one of the most distinctive voices in twentieth-century music. His characteristic sound, with brass and percussion well to the fore, might bring to mind a kind of English Hindemith mixed with Ives. The Gothic Symphony includes a setting of the *Te Deum*—compare with Mahler's first-movement *Veni Creator Spiritus.* Can it be coincidence that settings of great mythical or religious texts inspire composers to their grandest and most public creations?

GROUP 41

A. Stravinsky: *The Rite of Spring (1913)*
B. Prokofiev: Scythian Suite (1915)
1. Bartók: *The Miraculous Mandarin (1919)*
2. Varèse: *Amériques (1921–27)*
ALL

Stravinsky's quintessentially primitivist ballet directly inspired the Prokofiev, though the two sound quite different. In modern musical scholarship, Stravinsky occupies much the same place as Wagner does for students of the last century. Every syncopated rhythm or primal thud, each neoclassical essay or musical pastiche, seems to be traceable to his work. Naturally, this doesn't hold true in fact. Like Picasso, Stravinsky founded or invented practically nothing. But he did make copies that were often better than the originals, and he had many proselytizing disciples. His greatness isn't at all in doubt, though I firmly believe that equally great musical minds, such as Bartók's or Varèse's, could have come up with the same music had Stravinsky never existed.

All four works embody a paradox lying at the heart of most primitivist music: the more crudely barbaric the piece sounds, the more complex are the means employed in achieving the desired effect. Stravinsky, Prokofiev, and Varèse explore the primitivism of imaginary pagan and exotic cultures. Bartók's disturbing ballet captures the cruelty and barbarism of modern life in the city—a concrete jungle. These pieces are not for people with sensitive ears or intolerant neighbors.

GROUP 42
A. Tchaikovsky: *Symphony No. 6 ("Pathétique") (1893)*
B. Rachmaninoff: *Symphony No. 1 (1895)*
1. Shostakovich: *Symphony No. 10 (1953)*
2. Prokofiev: *Symphony No. 5 (1944)*
ALL

The Russian symphony holds a place of pride in the orchestral repertory. Shameless emotional intensity, surging lyricism, and endless melancholy that usually manages a triumphant ending anyhow are all qualities that have endeared these works to a wide public.

Tchaikovsky's "Pathétique" and Rachmaninoff's First break the basic pattern, for the Tchaikovsky ends in a mood of blackest despair, while the Rachmaninoff concludes defiantly; the composer's motto for the work is "Vengeance is mine, I will repay." Heavy stuff, with the *Dies irae* naturally putting in an appearance.

Shostakovich's Tenth should have ended miserably as well, and indeed seems about ready to. But the sudden death of Stalin (who is portrayed by music of mindless aggression in the second movement) prompted the composer to his one genuinely giddy, happy finale. The four-note motive in the brass (first heard in the third movement) that trounces Stalin when he appears in the midst of the finale's festivities, is a musical acronym derived from the composer's initials. Chalk one up for artistic freedom.

Prokofiev's Fifth is his most popular symphony, written to inspire courage during World War II. His basically open and optimistic character contrasts sharply with Shostakovich's austere, uneasy introversion.

GROUP 43
A. Tippett: *Concerto for Double String Orchestra (1939)*
B. Britten: *Variations on a Theme by Frank Bridge (1937)*
1. Elgar: *Introduction and Allegro (1905)*
2. Bridge: *Suite for String Orchestra (1908)*
AB A1 B2

British composers seem to have a special affinity for the medium of string orchestra. Britten and Tippett (the latter still going strong) are the great English composers of the middle decades of this century. The theme borrowed by Britten does not come from Bridge's charming Suite, though it partakes of a similarly cool lyricism. Both Elgar and Tippett make use of contrapuntal devices, Elgar writing a grand, fugal development, and Tippett building on the polyphony of the English Renaissance masters (see Group 37). Britten's more cosmopolitan set of variations includes a series of witty parodies, among them a twittering operatic soprano and a morosely Mahlerian funeral march (see Group 27).

GROUP 44
A. Bartók: *Music for Strings, Percussion,*
and Celesta (1936)
B. Chávez: *Sinfonía India (1935)*
1. Martinů: *Double Concerto for Two String Orchestras,*
Piano, and Timpani (1938)
2. Ives: *Three Places in New England (1908)*
AB A1 B2 A2

Chávez's colorful and brash *Sinfonía India*, compared with the magnificent Bartók piece, illustrates the difference between a musical idiom that has assimilated ethnic elements, and one in which those elements constitute the principal justification for the composition. Though he was later to evolve an integrated musical language very similar to Bartók's, in this early work of Chávez Mexican folk sounds and rhythms dominate. By contrast, the Hungarian music opening Bartók's finale sets in relief the complex preceding developments, and provides a necessary emotional release.

Martinů's Double Concerto is, like the Bartók, a tough but very gratifying work, and it employs antiphonal strings with timpani and piano in remarkably similar fashion. Ives' *Three Places* celebrates the sights and sounds of New England just as Chávez exults in his native Mexico. The second movement, with its two unsynchronized brass bands crashing into one another is hilariously cacophonous. In the finale, which depicts the distant strains of a church hymn carried on billowing river mists, Ives creates one of the most poetic moments in all music.

GROUP 45
A. Mahler: *Kindertotenlieder*
(Songs on the Death of Children) (1904)
B. Holst: *Savitri* (1908)
1. Berlioz: *Les nuits d'été (Summer Nights)* (1841)
2. Britten: *The Turn of the Screw* (1954)
AB A1 B2

Many of the same composers known for their exploitation of the largest instrumental forces simultaneously found satisfaction in writing for chamber orchestra. Mahler's ultimately consoling song cycle is a miracle of orchestral beauty and economy. Holst's chamber opera, for double string quartet, two flutes, English horn, and double bass, tells the Hindu legend of a woman who cheats death into restoring the life of her husband. Only thirty minutes long, *Savitri* is one of Holst's most nearly perfect creations.

Berlioz's gorgeous songs were not orchestrated and collected until some time after their original composition. Though not conceived as a cycle, they clearly inspired Mahler to his efforts in the medium. Britten's chamber opera sets Henry James' ghost story in what is undoubtedly one of the finest pieces of contemporary musical theater. Nothing is small about it save the forces required. Britten has cast the music as a theme and variations, each of which determines the character of the individual scenes.

GROUP 46
A. Saint-Saëns: *Symphony No. 3 ("Organ") (1886)*
B. Chausson: *Symphony in B-flat (1890)*
1. Dukas: *Symphony in C (1896)*
2. Roussel: *Symphony No. 2 (1921)*
ALL

French composers normally avoid writing symphonies for the simple reason that they are the sort of thing those dull and pedantic Germans do. Needless to say, the French are jealous. And so, despite their natural antipathy, they occasionally take the plunge, albeit with a twist. Saint-Saëns links his four movements into two pairs, incorporates a piano and an organ, and has a motto theme that recurs in each movement.

All three of the other works under consideration employ three movements instead of the usual four. Chausson's music exhibits a moody, emotional intensity that brings to mind the Russians (see Group 42). The Dukas has Chausson's structure with Saint-Saëns' suave clarity. Notice that both Chausson and Dukas, writing "absolute" music, abjure the exotic percussion and coloristic effects characteristic of the French school. In short, they sound at times a bit German. In a musical culture that so welcomes outside influences, it might only be expected that there should be a Germanic strain in French music. And so there is. But nationalistic pride has prevented these fine works from gaining the attention that they deserve.

Roussel was a born symphonist. In his Second Symphony, you can actually hear him evolving a unique symphonic voice of his own. Orchestral sounds that are classically French (such as the writing for harp and percussion in the second movement), go hand in hand with solidly symphonic developments.

GROUP 47

A. Bach: *Concerto for Four Harpsichords (1723)*
B. Vivaldi: *Concerto for Four Violins, Op. 3, No. 10 (1712)*
1. Bach: *Concerto for Two Harpsichords in C minor,*
BWV 1062 (1723)
2. Bach: *Concerto for Two Violins in D minor (1723)*
AB A1 B2 12

In the jolly days before copyright, composers freely borrowed from each other. Often, arrangements had to be made to adapt music to local circumstances, and most composers would have actually been flattered to see their music selected for transcription. After all, what better proof could there be of a work's popularity?

There are really only two pieces listed above. Bach's quadruple concerto is a transcription of Vivaldi's. And while the Bach double violin concerto allows you to compare his violin music with that of his Italian contemporary (and see Group 5), you can also hear how Bach transcribes himself for two harpsichords. For additional fun, why not try the Double Harpsichord Concerto in C, BWV 1061, which as far as anyone can tell was not a transcription? How does this supposedly genuine keyboard music differ from violin-based transcription, and how do the copies differ from the originals?

GROUP 4 8
A. Mendelssohn: *Italian Symphony (1833)*
B. Berlioz: *Harold in Italy (Chapter 9) (1834)*
1. Berwald: *Symphonie singulière (1845)*
2. Bernstein: *Symphony No. 2*
("The Age of Anxiety") (1949)
AB A1 B2

Mendelssohn hated Berlioz, so it's only fair that you should have a chance to hear the two in close proximity, on a similar subject. The Italian Symphony has elegance and charm, and a refined fastidiousness (listen to the trio in the third movement, with its fussy trumpets and drums) that goes far in explaining Mendelssohn's abhorrence of his uninhibited contemporary. Berlioz's *Harold,* after Byron, is a concertante symphony for viola and orchestra. The Mendelssohn sounds more Italian, but then again, the Berlioz is about the person more than the place.

Franz Berwald was a Swedish contemporary of Mendelssohn, very much of the same school, though he was more formally and harmonically adventurous. His symphony contains a scherzo within its slow movement, and the characterful wind writing establishes Berwald as the first composer whose music can recognizably be called Nordic (see Group 30).

Bernstein's jazzy Second Symphony, based on the Auden poem of the same title, proves that the concertante symphony is alive and well even today. The soloist in this case plays the piano. Like Berlioz's *Harold,* the solo's involvement diminishes as the work proceeds.

GROUP 49

A. Bruckner: *Symphony No. 7*
B. Franck: *Symphony in D minor*
1. Sibelius: *Symphony No. 3*
2. Magnard: *Symphony No. 4*

AB A1 B2

Bruckner and Franck were both famous organists, and also devout Roman Catholics. Some commentators hear in their music a predilection for organlike sounds, especially in the way both composers pit massed sections of the orchestra against each other. I tend to disagree with this view, but you can make up your own mind.

Franck's single symphony, with its rich, chromatic (see Group 22) harmonies and recurring themes (cyclic form—see Group 54) spawned a whole crowd of similar pieces by Chausson, Dukas, Roussel (see Group 46), and later Albéric Magnard, who reverts to the more traditional four-movement form. The Fourth Symphony is a serious, even noble work that deserves much wider currency. Its motto theme appears at the beginning as a gleam of light on harp and piccolo, and returns like a beacon of salvation on the trumpets twice during the finale, before leading the piece to a tranquil close.

Bruckner, unlike Franck, created no school, but he shares certain fascinating traits with Sibelius. First, both composers disliked orchestral violins (remarkable in Sibelius's case, considering his wonderful concerto for the instrument). They usually give the bulk of their thematic material either to woodwinds (Sibelius), brass (Bruckner), or lower strings, especially cellos (both). Second, there's a marked preference for unmixed instrumental colors, in which winds and brass play over shifting string textures. Harmonically, both men often prefer archaic, sometimes modal sounds. Compare the dancelike third subject of Bruckner's first movement with the second subject of Sibelius's (both introduced by large brass climaxes, and consisting of repeated melodic cells over a simple accompaniment). And note the grand, almost prayerful Amens that conclude both of these movements. Of course, there are differences too. Like the Franck (but not to the same degree), Bruckner's Seventh is broadly cyclical. The opening themes of the first and last movements are closely related, and the codas are practically identical.

And then there is the question of time-scale. Sibelius was a master of fluidly changing tempos and concise musical forms. Bruckner's cathedrals in sound move at a pace even slower than Wagner's. Nevertheless, the similarities are significant and curious. Might they stem from a shared preference for impersonal musical materials (see Chapter 10)?

GROUP 50
A. Mahler: *Symphony No. 9 (1909)*
B. Ravel: *Daphnis et Chloé (Chapter 9) (1912)*
1. Nielsen: *Symphony No. 5 (1922)*
2. Roussel: *Bacchus and Ariadne (complete) (1930)*
AB A1 B2

Mahler and Ravel were aesthetic opposites, yet their two works begin very similarly: a harp phrase, a horn theme, some hesitant melodic fragments. Both composers build their musical structures from these motives, yet the Mahler is "symphonic" and the Ravel merely "episodic." Ravel's themes recur at crucial points as transitions, to bind his sections together. Mahler's first movement grows organically from its quiet opening, and his themes are the actual subjects of the discourse. They comprise the melodic fabric, evolving different facets according to the emotional climate of the music. Ravel's motives almost never change anything other than instrumentation. Try to get a feel for the distinction between these two types of musical construction.

The first movement of Nielsen's Fifth shares a basic conceptual principal with Mahler's: both feature a titanic struggle against the forces of negation and hostility. Listen to each composer interpret this battle in his own terms. Nielsen ultimately triumphs while Mahler finally succumbs, but note that both first movements end in a spirit of exhausted tranquillity, their energies utterly spent.

Roussel's *Bacchus* is, like *Daphnis,* a ballet based on a classical Greek subject. As a mature work by France's greatest symphonist (don't miss his magnificent Third Symphony in Group 15), would you say that it is more symphonic than the Ravel?

GROUP 51
A. Copland: *Symphony No. 3 (1946)*
B. Harris: *Symphony No. 3 (1937)*
1. Martinů: *Symphony No. 4 (1945)*
2. Piston: *Symphony No. 6 (1955)*
ALL

Like the French, American composers have approached the symphony with trepidation. In the nineteenth century, when Germanic tastes dominated American musical culture, composers produced lots of pseudo-Brahms, very conservative in idiom. But in this century, Paris was the center of musical culture around which young American artists gathered, most notably Piston, Copland, and Harris.

But what is Martinů, a Czech, doing here? Well, he studied in Paris, too, at the same time as the Americans. His six symphonies were all written in the United States, and he shares with Copland, Piston, and Harris a love of simple, almost folklike themes coupled with springy, athletic rhythms and a spacious orchestral sonority. In their slow movements, all four composers adopt a chromatic, but still instrumentally lean sound. In fact, you can even hear the Marlboro man gallop through the closing pages of Martinů's Fourth!

Walter Piston was a musical pedagogue of world renown. His textbooks are still in standard use, but it is his superbly crafted, perennially fresh music that ought to be standard listening. The finale of the Sixth, like much in the other composers, has that special sound we have come to associate with cowboys and the Old West.

GROUP 52
A. Haydn: *Symphony No. 93 (1792)*
B. Beethoven: *Symphony No. 8 (1812)*
1. Mahler: *Symphony No. 4 (1900)*
2. Shostakovich: *Symphony No. 9 (1945)*
ALL

In Group 1, we compared two Classical works to two imitations, one an affectionate tribute, the other in a beautiful but immature style. What do we mean when we speak of the Classical period, and why do we call it that? Simply because, as with the Elizabethan theater of Shakespeare's time, cultural, social, and political forces combined to produce a universal style in which all the constituent elements share in a state of perfect equilibrium. Like a Shakespearean comedy, Haydn's 93rd Symphony contains the most exquisite wit next to some genuinely bawdy clowning (the slow movement invents the musical equivalent of the whoopee cushion). Haydn manages to be at once learned and popular, elegant yet affecting.

With Beethoven, the Classical style passes away, and his Eighth Symphony seems to be a farewell of the best kind: a deliberate evocation of the earlier style by one who attained complete mastery in that style, and carried it forward to new heights.

Nevertheless, each age has produced works in which unselfconscious ease of expression, conveyed through a mastery of complex form so complete as to make each moment sound inevitable, qualifies them as Classical in the Haydnesque sense. Mahler's Fourth and Shostakovich's Ninth are two such works, not surprisingly their respective composers' most lighthearted. They have to be, for the Classical style, as you can hear for yourself, is the epitome of balance, both musically and emotionally.

GROUP 53

A. Brahms: *Piano Trio in C minor (1886)*
B. Dvořák: *Piano Trio in F minor (Chapter 7) (1883)*
1. Chausson: *Piano Trio in G minor (1881)*
2. Novák: *Piano Trio in D minor (1902)*
AB A1 B2

Here are four magnificent piano trios, each exploring in its unique way the tragic atmosphere of minor keys. Brahms and Dvořák have been compared before in the context of orchestral music (Groups 8 and 22), and comparison is equally rewarding in the field of chamber composition. Dvořák's trio is one of the largest works for this combination in the repertoire, as well as one of his most richly emotional and tragic statements. It's entirely possible that this masterpiece spurred Brahms to produce his greatest trio, which like Beethoven's Fifth follows a musical progression from tragedy to triumph. Dvořák's final moments, though major, appear far more equivocal.

Vítězslav Novák was one of Dvořák's most gifted pupils, and his D-minor Trio remains a remarkable work in several respects. It's one of those rare occurrences, a piece that remains in the minor key up to the very end, expiring pathetically in a mood of utter darkness. Along the way, Novák manages to combine the four movements of the typical large-scale instrumental composition into one compact, tightly developed musical structure.

Chausson's trio represents a significant moment in French musical history. The decade of the 1870s, following the Franco-Prussian War, was one of great economic hardship in France. Opera, the unchallenged focus of French music throughout the nineteenth century, lost some of its preeminence as theaters were forced to close for lack of revenue. The practical upshot of this climate was the possibility that composers could focus on creating a French school of instrumental music. Of course, German music provided the obvious model, and Chausson's trio, an early work, certainly owes something to Beethoven and Brahms (whose C-minor Trio was actually his third and last), but as in the Novák, the minor-key ending is certainly unusual. Determining the extent of these influences is a task I leave to you.

GROUP 54
A. Magnard: *Violin Sonata (1901)*
B. Fauré: *Violin Sonata No. 2 (1917)*
1. Franck: *Violin Sonata (1886)*
2. Debussy: *Violin Sonata (1917)*
AB A1 B2

The French are to culture what the Japanese are to automobiles, and this applies particularly in music. These four violin sonatas represent the French art of chamber music composition at its most completely mature. One of the stranger results of Wagner's influence on European music is that while German composers started churning out operas in the latter half of the nineteenth century, the French took up the hitherto almost exclusively Germanic challenge of instrumental music. Like the Japanese today, they refined the basic concept, making something new and, through sheer craftsmanship, often superior to the home-grown product.

Magnard and Fauré represent two French solutions to the formal challenge of chamber music. Magnard's sonata is a four-movement work in cyclical form (that is, with a recurring theme that permeates the various movements and binds them together). Its not-too-distant ancestor is Franck's sonata, which has a finale with a tune so haunting it will stick in your head for life. Fauré's sonata shares with Debussy a three-movement structure that highlights the French love of concision and balance, along with that haunting, elusive, and rhapsodic quality that places both pieces among their respective composers' last efforts.

GROUP 55

A. Brahms: *Clarinet Quintet (1891)*
B. Brahms: *Clarinet Sonata No. 1 (1894)*
1. Mozart: *Clarinet Quintet (1789)*
2. Poulenc: *Clarinet Sonata (1962)*
AB A1 B2 12

The combination of clarinet with string quartet (as in the quintets) or clarinet and piano (the sonatas) has produced numerous attractive pieces, among which these four are probably the finest. Brahms fell in love with the clarinet at the end of his life, and the sharper tone of the wind instrument gives his often autumnal, sometimes enigmatic inspiration a clear but mellow sound. His quintet is a clear tribute to Mozart, whose writing for the clarinet can be said to have "discovered" the instrument. Mozart's own quintet enjoyed a particular burst of popularity after its use in the final episode of the television show "M*A*S*H." Poulenc's sonata is dedicated to the memory of his friend the composer Arthur Honegger, and also owes Mozart a debt in terms of elegance and fastidious reserve. In fact, all four works have a very potent, elegiac quality about them that seems uniquely suited to the liquid tones of the clarinet.

GROUP 56

A. Mozart: *Piano and Wind Quintet, K. 452 (1784)*
B. Beethoven: *Piano and Wind Quintet, Op. 16 (1796)*
   1. Thuille: *Piano and Wind Sextet, Op. 6 (1888)*
   2. Magnard: *Piano and Wind Quintet, Op. 8 (1894)*
AB A1 B2

I include opus numbers to highlight a curious fact. All four works listed above are early. Of course, anything that Mozart wrote after the age of fifteen can be considered mature, but he was still only twenty-eight when he composed his quintet for piano, oboe, clarinet, bassoon and horn, and he considered it his finest work up to that point. Beethoven's quintet is clearly based on Mozart's. German composer Ludwig Thuille adds a flute to his ensemble, but otherwise fashions a work of Mozartean elegance and charm in its own, Romantic way. Magnard, by contrast, takes up Beethoven's stormier challenge, yet has room for the humor and relaxed atmosphere that seem an integral part of writing for wind instruments. This combination is particularly difficult as regards balance and ensemble, so perhaps it's not surprising that young composers test their skills with it on the road to perfecting their craft, while at the same time making some delightful music.

GROUP 57

A. Szymanowski: *Myths for Violin and Piano (1915)*
B. Bloch: *Violin Sonata No. 2 ("Poème Mystique") (1924)*
1. Villa-Lobos: *Quintet for Flute, Harp,
and String Trio (1957)*
2. Scriabin: *Poem of Ecstasy (1908)*
AB A1 B2

In Groups 12 and 31 we had an opportunity to look at orchestral music evocative of exotic subjects, or inspired by Orientalism and Eastern philosophy. These same interests produced some marvelous chamber music, too, as the violin and piano works of Bloch and Szymanowski demonstrate. Villa-Lobos's luscious quintet, though lacking the programmatic titles of Szymanowski's *Myths,* conjures up its tropical Brazilian origins with great musical specificity. Scriabin's famous symphonic poem, though an orchestral work scored for huge forces, is like the Bloch sonata a single-movement composition full of sensuous yearning. Bloch's chamber setting is more intimate, Scriabin's orchestral phantasmagoria more overwhelming. Which appeals to you more?

GROUP 58

A. Brahms: *Piano Quintet (1864)*
B. Fauré: *Piano Quintet No. 1 (1906)*
1. Dohnányi: *Piano Quintet No. 1 (1895)*
2. Dohnányi: *Sextet for Piano, Horn,
Clarinet and String Trio (1935)*
AB A1 A2 12

Brahms and Fauré were two of the three great composers of chamber music in the second half of the nineteenth century (the third was Dvořák). The two piano quintets compared here show both musicians at their most individual. Brahms' fiery and passionate drama requires the standard four movements, while Fauré's refined lyricism involves only three. Although both composers employ the minor mode, the contrast in spirit could hardly be greater.

Dohnányi's two compositions show him moving away from the Brahmsian piano quintet of his early years, a piece which the German master himself admired, to a more individual style based on cyclical themes, French style, and a thoroughly engaging sense of humor. The finale of the sextet is one of the most witty and characterful creations in the Romantic repertoire.

GROUP 59
A. Chopin: *Etudes* (1829–37)
B. Schumann: *Symphonic Etudes* (1837)
1. Debussy: *Etudes* (1915)
2. Bach: *Two- and Three-Part Inventions* (1723)
ALL

All the pieces in this group embrace the same concept: music designed to perfect keyboard technique, while at the same time maintaining the highest artistic standards. There are not many examples of "teaching" pieces which at the same time exhibit the poetry and musical depth necessary to become mainstays of the repertoire, but here are the exceptions. Bach is the foremost practitioner of this art, and the Inventions have challenged budding pianists for over two and a half centuries, beginning with Bach's own children. Chopin and Schumann, friends and contemporaries, carried piano composition to new heights of virtuosity in their sets of Etudes. Schumann's set, as well as being cast in variation form, is "symphonic" to the extent that he deliberately pursues new colors and sounds, treating the piano as a potential orchestra. Chopin's Etudes, in two books of twelve, each piece a short masterpiece in miniature, clearly inspired Debussy's dozen pianistic gems.

GROUP 60
A. Dvořák: *Quartet No. 10 (1878)*
B. Smetana: *Quartet No. 1 (1876)*
1. Moeran: *Quartet (1921)*
2. Borodin: *Quartet No. 2 (1885)*
AB A1 B2

Musical nationalism produced much attractive instrumental music, whether Czech (Group 26), British (Group 32), or Russian (Group 42). Smetana's dramatic first quartet carries the autobiographical subtitle "From My Life," and the first violin squeal at the end of the finale represents the first symptoms of the composer's sudden deafness. Dvořák's quartet, by contrast, is as sunny and relaxed a work as any in the repertoire. Moeran's equally lyrical and folk-inspired quartet of 1921 serves as the British equivalent of Dvořák's pastoral holiday, while Smetana's Slavic inflections find their Russian counterparts in Borodin's lovely Second Quartet.

GROUP 61
A. Ravel: *Piano Trio (1914)*
B. Debussy: *Trio for Flute, Harp, and Viola (1916)*
1. Debussy: *Piano Trio (ca. 1880)*
2. Koechlin: *Quintette Primavera for Flute, Harp, and String Trio (1934)*
AB A1 B2 B1

Debussy and Ravel, in Group 38, appear together in Spanish dress. Here they are each their own remarkable selves, in some ways at their most extreme. Ravel's trio is a celebration of rhythm, the second movement (called "Pantoum") actually modeled on metrical poetry. Debussy's trio practically negates rhythm in favor of flickering, hazy washes of sound. For once musical "impressionism" lives up to its name. Koechlin's quintet is another in a unique series of chamber works with harp that are a French specialty. As the title implies, the music has a springlike freshness which, particularly in its second movement, stands comparison with Debussy's opening "Pastorale." Debussy's early piano trio was only rediscovered in 1982. Although the work owes an obvious debt to German models, the second movement has a remarkably Ravelian delicacy and charm. Comparison of the two Debussy trios reveals the subtlety of the composer's late style in light of one of his earliest musical experiments.

GROUP 62
A. Haydn: *Quartet, Op. 33, No. 2 ("Joke") (1781)*
B. Haydn: *Sonata in E-flat (Hoboken No. 52;*
Landon No. 62) (1794)
1. Poulenc: *Trio for Piano, Oboe, and Bassoon (1926)*
2. Beethoven: *Sonata No. 21 ("Waldstein") (1804)*
AB A1 B2

Haydn's significance as a composer of chamber music is even greater than as a composer of orchestral music, if such a thing were possible. He invented the string quartet, and his achievement in this medium remains in many ways unsurpassed. The six quartets of Opus 33 evidence for the first time in Classical chamber music the love of comedy that was to characterize so many of the pieces that followed. In this particular case, the joke lies in the theme of the finale. See if you can tell when the quartet actually ends.

Haydn's E-flat Sonata of 1794 is the greatest work of its kind before Beethoven. The wit and humor of the earlier quartet appear here, wedded to an imposing sense of scale and, in the slow movement, a deeply lyrical strain. Beethoven's magnificent Waldstein Sonata expands the E-flat Sonata's heroic and lyrical dimensions without sacrificing wit, while Poulenc's charming trio, openly modeled on Haydn in the first movement, combines warmth and charm in a manner utterly typical of both composers.

GROUP 63
A. Beethoven: *Sonata Quasi una Fantasia,*
Op. 27, No. 2 ("Moonlight") (1801)
B. Schubert: *Fantasie in C ("Wanderer") (1822)*
1. Mozart: *Fantasia in C minor (1785)*
2. Liszt: *Sonata in B minor (1853)*
AB A1 B2

A fantasia, or fantasy, as the title implies, usually means a composition in more or less free style, but in any event less strict than a sonata. True to form, Beethoven's Moonlight Sonata only really develops the tensions characteristic of sonata form in the last of its three movements, while Mozart's single-movement fantasia alternates a series of improvisatory episodes in contrasting tempos. Schubert's Wanderer Fantasie, by contrast, is one of his most tightly organized pieces. Its single movement subdivides into the standard four contrasting sections of the Classical sonata, and all are based on thematic material derived from the composer's earlier song "The Wanderer." Liszt, fresh from making a transcription for piano and orchestra of Schubert's solo piano original, based his sonata on the structure of the Wanderer Fantasie. Just a few basic themes serve to build up the entire thirty-minute-long piece.

GROUP 64
A. Alkan: *Grande Sonate* (1847)
B. Chopin: *Sonata No. 2* (1839)
1. Ravel: *Gaspard de la nuit* (1908)
2. Rachmaninoff: *Sonata No. 1* (1907)
AB A1 B2 B1

The Alkan and Chopin piano sonatas represent a sort of high noon in Romantic keyboard music. Not only are their formal structures fresh and masterly, but both works display a passionate morbidity that at times becomes almost expressionistic. Chopin's sonata contains the instantly recognizable funeral march that has made the piece famous, preceding an enigmatic finale that is a musical expression of nihilistic terror. Alkan's sonata ends with a funeral march subtitled "Prometheus Bound," while each of its four movements becomes progressively slower.

Rachmaninoff's first sonata, in three substantial movements, shares much of Chopin's turbulent melancholy on its way to a finale that reveals the *Dies irae* chant from the Requiem Mass as the music's final destination. Ravel's *Gaspard de la nuit* takes the Romantic tradition as the basis for a pianistic essay in the macabre. "Ondine," the water sprite of the first movement, appears seductive in her efforts to lure men to their deaths. "Le Gibet," close relative to the funeral music of Chopin and Alkan, depicts a corpse swinging on the scaffold. "Scarbo," an evil gnome, lurches about to music that at times recalls the Satanic elements of Alkan's second movement, subtitled "Quasi-Faust." "Scarbo" also has the reputation of being among the most notoriously difficult pieces ever written for the piano.

GROUP 65
A. Chopin: *Waltzes (1829–47)*
B. Chopin: *Twenty-four Preludes (1839)*
1. Alwyn: *Fantasy Waltzes (1956)*
2. Debussy: *Préludes: Books I and II (1910–13)*
AB A1 B2

Chopin's waltzes were composed when the waltz was actually danced to. This is important to keep in mind at present, when we generally hear nineteenth-century dance music only in a concert context. They are poetic stylizations of the popular music being played in dance halls. William Alwyn's Fantasy Waltzes are thus, in a sense, twice removed from the original, since they were clearly composed in the full light of Chopin's pathbreaking achievements. They radiate a sense of wistful nostalgia for a world long since forgotten.

A prelude, as the word suggests, is supposed to introduce something—in the Baroque period usually a fugue. Chopin's Preludes, in all the major and minor keys, are clearly meant to be played as a single work. Each is a miniature tone picture complete in itself, yet too brief to really stand alone. Debussy's Préludes, by contrast, are pianistic program works. In vintage preludial fashion, the title of each piece appears in the score *after* the music itself. Listen first, then see what Debussy had on his mind. The famous "Girl with the Flaxen Hair" puts in an appearance, but I won't give away precisely where.

GROUP 66
A. Clarke: *Piano Trio (1921)*
B. Bridge: *Piano Trio No. 2 (1929)*
1. Martinů: *Piano Quintet No. 2 (1944)*
2. Shostakovich: *Piano Trio No. 2 (1944)*
AB A1 B2 A2

Rebecca Clarke and Frank Bridge are both excellent British composers who are less well known than they should be, probably because Clarke was a woman, and because Bridge's late style owes nothing to any nationalistic school. Clarke's trio is a tough and passionate piece that acquires a spiky, folk-influenced dance character in its third (final) movement. This style, in which folk influences have become fully integrated into a uniquely personal style also characterizes Martinů's second piano quintet, though there the inspiration is Czech.

Frank Bridge's second trio is a deeply disturbing work. The music remains tonally ambiguous throughout, the writing for piano and strings often very thin and widely spaced (as is also the case in the Shostakovich). Much of the music can best be described as "spacy." And yet, it's also a very haunting, almost refreshing piece, full of fascinating sounds and rhythms. Shostakovich's trio expresses a similar feeling of foreboding by alternating passages of numb stillness with tortured fragments of Jewish dance music that, in the finale, becomes almost unbearably tragic. Like the Bridge, elements of earlier movements recur at the end on the way to a quiet close. It's also worthwhile to compare the last movements of the Clarke and Shostakovich trios for the ways in which both artists employ folk music and dance elements to very different ends.

GROUP 67
A. Beethoven: *Violin Sonata No. 9 ("Kreutzer") (1803)*
B. Beethoven: *Quartet No. 7 (Rasumovsky No. 1) (1806)*
1. Fauré: *Violin Sonata No. 1 (1875)*
2. Janáček: *Quartet No. 1 ("Kreutzer Sonata") (1924)*
AB A1 B2 A2

These two works of Beethoven's early middle period represent the kind of musical expansion that he was bringing to the Classical forms. Although his reputation rests to some extent on the storm and stress of pieces like the Fifth Symphony, Beethoven was equally adept at the dazzling virtuosity of the Kreutzer Sonata and the calm strength of the Seventh Quartet. Beethoven composed three quartets for Count Rasumovsky, who requested that each contain a Russian theme; in this case, the theme appears in the finale.

The presence of Janáček's quartet requires a bit of explanation. The subtitle comes from Tolstoy's story, which is in turn named after the Beethoven sonata. But there's some musical point too, just in case you don't feel like reading Tolstoy. Janáček's two quartets are great masterpieces of the medium, full of fresh sounds and strong rhythms. Much of the physical drive and virtuosity of the Kreutzer Sonata's first movement finds a counterpart in Janáček's quartet writing.

What about Fauré's lovely sonata? Like Beethoven, Fauré reached his early maturity in the field of chamber music. Only Brahms and Franck in the second half of the nineteenth century composed violin sonatas as successful, and theirs came later. Beethoven's example, then, is most important, and this sonata announces the presence of a major new voice in chamber music with characteristic skill and reticence.

GROUP 68
A. Brahms/Schoenberg: *Piano Quartet No. 1 (1937)*
B. Bach/Elgar: *Fantasy and Fugue in C minor (1922)*
1. Brahms: *Piano Quartet No. 1 (1861)*
2. Bach: *Organ Fantasy and Fugue in C minor, BWV 537 (ca. 1710)*
AB A1 B2

In the Classical period, music publishers used to print chamber transcriptions of symphonic works. Performance in the home was the only way to hear most orchestral music when public concerts were almost nonexistent. Romantic and modern composers, on the other hand, have had a field day transcribing for enormous orchestras more intimate works by earlier masters. Here are two. You'll find listening to them great fun, particularly since it's relatively certain that Bach and Brahms would have had heart attacks if they could have heard what Schoenberg and Elgar actually did to their music. The gypsy finale of the Brahms becomes an instrumental orgy, with xylophones, glockenspiels, elephantine tubas—the whole works. Elgar's Bach, on the other hand, by virtue of some wild writing for tambourine, harp, and brass becomes a sort of Baroque counterpart to his "March of the Mogul Emperors" from *The Crown of India Suite*. It's all great fun in a refreshingly vulgar sort of way.

GROUP 69

A. Dvořák: *Quartet No. 12, Op. 96 ("American") (1893)*
B. Dvořák: *String Quintet in E-flat, Op. 97 (1893)*
1. Janáček: *Quartet No. 2 ("Intimate Pages") (1928)*
2. Bruckner: *String Quintet (1879–84)*
AB A1 B2

During his stay in America, Dvořák composed two chamber works that number among his most popular. Both explore and refine the Czech master's interest in pentatonic (scales of five-notes) melody, and Dvořák himself claimed to have been inspired by hearing Negro spirituals and what he considered to be "Indian" rhythms. In fact, both pieces were written during his stay in a Czech community in Iowa, and the elements that Dvořák may or may not have borrowed are so close to the purely Slavic music he habitually wrote as to make no difference. Nevertheless, these two magnificent works focus on pentatonic melodies and zippy rhythms to an unprecedented extent, taking the composer farther away from his Germanic roots.

Janáček's Second Quartet is one of the glories of the modern quartet literature, and expresses the composer's infatuation with a woman thirty-eight years his junior. Its Slavic intensity and unique ensemble sound make it one of the most rewarding pieces in the repertoire, especially for listeners new to chamber music. Bruckner's quintet is a solitary masterpiece, the composer's only mature chamber work. It contains one of the great slow movements in Romantic chamber music, and greatly rewards repeated hearings. Like the Dvořák, it is one of the few great string quintets written in the nineteenth century (the others are by Schubert and Brahms).

GROUP 70
A. Rachmaninoff: *Rhapsody on a Theme by Paganini (Chapter 6) (1934)*
B. Dohnányi: *Variations on a Nursery Tune (1914)*
1. Brahms: *Paganini Variations (Books 1 and 2) (1862–63)*
2. Mozart: *Variations on "Ah, vous dirai-je, maman,"* K. 265 (1781)
AB A1 B2

Rachmaninoff and Dohnányi have each composed masterpieces in variation form for piano and orchestra. Mozart and Brahms write variations on the same tunes as Dohnányi and Rachmaninoff, respectively, but for piano alone. Here is an excellent opportunity for comparison. The Paganini theme comes from No. 24 of his Caprices for solo violin, and you might want to give it a listen as well, since Paganini also treats it as a subject for variations. The Mozart and Dohnányi tune will be instantly familiar to everyone, and by giving it away I'd be ruining the point of Dohnányi's orchestral introduction. But believe me, you've heard it before.

GROUP 71
A. Mozart: *String Quintet, K. 614 (1791)*
B. Mozart: *Quartet, K. 421 (1783)*
1. Schubert: *String Quintet, D. 956 (1828)*
2. Schubert: *Quartet No. 14 ("Death and the Maiden") (1824)*
AB A1 B2 12

If Haydn invented the string quartet, to Mozart must go the credit for, if not inventing, then in all events perfecting the string quintet. His five mature quintets are his greatest chamber works, and their comparative neglect is unaccountable. Mozart's quartets, by contrast, are better known, especially his set of six dedicated to his friend Haydn. The D-minor Quartet is one of these. Its tense, melancholy atmosphere sets the stage for the musical Romanticism that blossoms forth in Schubert's quartet in the same key. Schubert's quintet shares with Mozart's the distinction, if it can be called such, of having been composed in the last year of its composer's brief life. Mozart uses two violas, Schubert two cellos, and comparing the basic sound of both pieces that results from the choice of instruments is interesting and, as always, musically rewarding.

GROUP 72

A. Haydn: *Sonata No. 33 in C minor (1771)*
B. Haydn: *Symphony No. 44 ("Mourning") (ca. 1771)*
1. Beethoven: *Sonata No. 8 ("Pathétique") (1798)*
2. Strauss: *Death and Transfiguration (1890)*
AB A1 B2

In the late 1760s and early 1770s music (that is, Haydn and others) went through an emotional crisis which historians have named, after a novel of the period, Sturm und Drang (Storm and Stress). Many compositions of this period employ minor keys, even ending in them, and vent extraordinary feelings of rage and anxiety. Haydn's C-minor Sonata is the great keyboard work of his Sturm und Drang period, just as the Symphony No. 44 is one of several that embody this ethos.

Haydn was certainly not alone in going through a radical phase, emotionally speaking, early in his career. Beethoven's Pathétique Sonata is his answer to Haydn's (remember that "Pathétique" does not mean pathetic, but moody or dramatic), while Strauss' cosmic symphonic poem generates many of the same emotions as Haydn's symphony.

GROUP 73

A. Couperin: *Suite for Harpsichord No. 11 (Book 2) (1717)*
B. Bach: *Goldberg Variations (1742)*
1. Ravel: *Le tombeau de Couperin*
   (piano version) (1914–17)
2. Beethoven: *Diabelli Variations (1823)*
AB A1 B2

However difficult it may be to accustom yourself to the sound of the harpsichord, you should make the attempt. The Bach and Couperin pieces illustrate why. Both can be played on the piano, but particularly in the case of Couperin, the harpsichord allows a contrapuntal clarity and lightness of attack without sacrificing volume that this music seems to presume. As with Debussy's Preludes (Group 65), Couperin gives the short pieces that comprise his Eleventh Suite (or *Ordre*) fanciful titles. Bach's Goldberg Variations, by contrast, is a vast work potentially over an hour long (depending on repeats), and one of the two greatest sets of keyboard variations ever written. Beethoven's Diabelli Variations is the other.

When listening to the "Goldbergs," forget the theme, for the piece is actually closer to a passacaglia (see the discussion of Brahms' Fourth Symphony in Chapter 5), and the variations are based not on the tune, but the harmonies of the bass line. Beethoven's variations, by contrast, are frequently melodic, and the outline of the tune generally stays much more clearly in sight.

Ravel's tribute to the French Baroque, which translates as "Couperin's Tomb," follows an ancient musical custom of composing tributes to deceased composers. But Ravel uses the Baroque as more than an excuse for a neoclassical pastiche. The music expresses an innocence and nostalgia for things past that is all the more poignant if one recalls that each movement is dedicated to one of the composer's friends killed in World War I.

GROUP 74

A. Haydn: *Quartet in F, Op. 74, No. 2 (1793)*
B. Haydn: *Quartet in C, Op. 54, No. 2 (1787)*
1. Schubert: *Piano Trio No. 1 (1827)*
2. Bartók: *Quartet No. 6 (1939)*
AB A1 B2

These two Haydn quartets are typical of his mature genius. The F major is one of a set of six quartets (Opp. 73 and 74) written during his stay in London for the British public. This is music for concert performance, not the salon, and the music's bold thrust and folklike melodies aim at the widest possible audience. The C-major quartet, by contrast, is one of Haydn's most formally adventurous. The trio of the minuet, usually a lightly diverting dance, reveals some barely suppressed anguish. The finale begins as a slow movement, speeds up briefly, but concludes quietly in the slow tempo.

Schubert's trio has a first movement built on a remarkably similar plan to that of Haydn's F-major quartet. Listen to the opening moments in each work to see what I mean—to the "question and answer" cast of the phrases, alternately major and minor. Like the Haydn, Schubert's trio is a bold, "public" piece, positively radiating good spirits and healthy verve. Bartók's Sixth Quartet, on the other hand, is a lonely work. It begins with a tune marked "Sad," and this tune precedes every movement in increasing elaboration: first as a pure melody alone, then in two parts, then three, then finally as an entire slow finale with all four instruments participating.

Although the music of Haydn and Bartók is very different, try to get a sense of how each composer deploys his form (and emotional expression) in anticipation of a slow and quiet conclusion.

GROUP 75

A. Roussel: *Serenade for Flute, Harp,*
and String Trio (1925)
B. Kodály: *Serenade for Two Violins and Viola (1920)*
1. Ravel: *Introduction and Allegro for Flute, Clarinet,*
Harp, and String Quartet (1905)
2. Dohnányi: *Serenade for String Trio (1902)*
AB A1 B2

"Serenade" implies something lighter and less serious than "sonata," both formally and sometimes in terms of the instruments employed. For obvious reasons, composers like to spare themselves exposure to the pedantic scruples of musical scholars and critics when they write for unusual combinations of instruments, and the title "Serenade" covers any potential liability. But both the Roussel and Kodály are fully mature, beautifully crafted works that stand comparison with anything more "serious." Roussel's Serenade features the spiky harmonies and propulsive rhythms that characterize all of his later music. Kodály's demonstrates the composer's exhaustive study and affection for the folk music of his native Hungary.

Ravel's single movement, like the Roussel, is yet another piece in a genre that remains almost exclusively French: chamber music with harp. Dohnányi's Serenade is the work of a Hungarian composer, but unlike his compatriot Kodály, Dohnányi was content to remain within a Brahmsian idiom, only occasionally revealing folk influences.

GROUP 76
A. Tippett: *Symphony No. 1 (1945)*
B. Honegger: *Symphony No. 1 (1930)*
1. Shapero: *Symphony for Classical Orchestra (1947)*
2. Bloch: *Violin Sonata No. 1 (1920)*
AB A1 B2

Both Honegger and Tippett have fashioned symphonies based on propulsive rhythms and vigorous use of counterpoint. In each case, the various musical lines clash against each other with little regard for the rules of traditional harmony, and yet the result is very fresh and exhilarating. Harold Shapero's Symphony for Classical Orchestra has exactly the same orchestration as Beethoven's Fifth, deployed in the same way (trombones, piccolo, and contrabassoon in the finale only). As with the Tippett, the heart of the work is the slow movement, and both composers adhere to the traditions of their Classical predecessors in adopting the standard four-movement form. Shapero also shares with Tippett a love of intricate, syncopated rhythm, though within a less contrapuntally based style.

Bloch's First Violin Sonata makes a fascinating comparison with Honegger's symphony, since it has an absolutely identical form. Both first movements are violent and aggressive essays in brutal counterpoint, full of explosive rhythmic energy. The slow movements express an uneasy calm, frequently disturbed by moody, almost "blues-y" harmony. With three movements apiece, the finales of both compositions are marches that finally expire quietly, in total exhaustion.

GROUP 77

A. Haydn: *Mass in Time of War (1796)*
B. Haydn: *Te Deum (1800)*
1. Beethoven: *Missa solemnis (1823)*
2. Bruckner: *Te Deum (1884)*
AB A1 B2

Why listen to Latin Masses in the first place, no matter who wrote them? The answer, of course, is that the emotions expressed in the words are common to all whatever their religious affiliation, and, when set by a composer of genius, utterly universal. Contrast Haydn's Mass in Time of War, written with the Napoleonic Wars going full tilt, with the hymn of praise that is his *Te Deum.* Beethoven knew Haydn's Mass, and borrowed the concept of warlike sounds in the *Agnus Dei* as a contrast to the final plea for peace *(Dona nobis pacem).*

In all vocal music set to a sacred text, the form tends to follow the meaning of the words. Bruckner's *Te Deum,* an overpowering work that still sounds absolutely staggering (play it LOUD), unfolds like an enormous Gregorian chant for chorus, orchestra, and organ. And yet the form shows many similarities to Haydn's, though on a larger scale. Both works feature a quiet central episode at the words *Te ergo quaesumus* ("we therefore pray thee"), and conclude with mighty fugues.

GROUP 78
A. Verdi: *Requiem (1874)*
B. Brahms: *German Requiem (1867)*
1. Britten: *War Requiem (1962)*
2. Hindemith: *Requiem ("When Lilacs Last
in the Dooryard Bloom'd") (1946)*
AB A1 B2 12

You don't have to be a Catholic to write a Requiem, but it doesn't hurt, either. Neither Brahms nor Verdi was in any conventional way religious. In fact, both pretty much loathed organized religion in most of its forms. But when they needed to express publicly the sentiment of grief, they turned to texts which, not without reason, have embodied this sentiment down through the ages. Verdi sets the Latin Requiem Mass, while Brahms exhibits the Requiem idea in a setting of his own selection of words from the Bible.

Britten's War Requiem amplifies Verdi's approach by alternating the Latin text with the antiwar poems of Wilfred Owen, himself killed in World War I. Hindemith's Requiem follows Brahms' model, setting a text by Walt Whitman that was written as a tribute to President Lincoln after his assassination. The work is dedicated to the memory of President Franklin D. Roosevelt and to the American victims of World War II. The comparison between Hindemith and Britten is obvious, at least on extramusical grounds. It's interesting to note that settings of the Latin text, with its lines about the Day of Judgment (remember the *Dies irae?*), tend to be angrier and more dramatic than the comparatively elegiac and restrained compilations of Brahms and Hindemith.

GROUP 79
A. Haydn: *Lord Nelson Mass (1798)*
B. Cherubini: *Coronation Mass (1825)*
1. Janáček: *Glagolitic Mass (1926)*
2. Walton: *Coronation Te Deum (1953)*
AB A1 B2

Religion and politics meet in Cherubini's Coronation Mass, written for the enthronement of Charles X as king of France. The piece is supremely assured occasional music, and nothing could be more different from Cherubini's calmly confident Kyrie than the almost hysterical pleas for mercy that open Haydn's Lord Nelson Mass. Here is a work, religious or not, that takes full cognizance of a Europe that's far from peaceful. Particularly noteworthy is the Benedictus, where, in response to the text "Blessed is He who comes in the name of the Lord," trumpets and drums hammer out a violent fanfare that indicates that a suppliant, anno 1798, was anything but blessed.

Walton's *Te Deum,* another occasional piece, was written to celebrate the coronation of Queen Elizabeth II. I don't know if anyone ever asked her if she liked it or not, but she certainly should have. Janáček's Glagolitic Mass was so named for the text, which is in Old Church Slavonic. Since the composer regarded churches as symbols of death, and refused to have anything to do with organized religion, he regarded his Mass as a hymn in praise of the Czech nation. Call it what you will, the piece is one of this century's greatest, most fascinating, and sonically exciting choral works. Notice the similarities to Haydn in some of the text settings, especially the anguished Kyrie, featuring in both cases extended soprano solos.

GROUP 80
A. Bach: *Italian Concerto (1735)*
B. Bach: *Triple Concerto (ca. 1730)*
1. Alkan: *Concerto for Piano Solo (Nos. 8–10 from Twelve Etudes, Op. 39) (1857)*
2. Beethoven: *Triple Concerto (1804)*
AB A1 B2

Bach's Italian Concerto perfectly embodies the concerto principle, and yet is written for solo harpsichord. The right hand is the soloist, the left hand the accompaniment, and the two together form the orchestra. Even though the Triple Concerto has three soloists—flute, violin, and harpsichord—its form is based on exactly the same concepts as the Italian Concerto. Listen and hear for yourself.

Alkan's concerto for solo piano is the Romantic answer to Bach's concerto for harpsichord alone. Here, the pianist must create quasi-orchestral textures within a broad sonata framework: the first movement alone lasts nearly half an hour. The piece is one of the great tours de force of the Romantic period, and its three movements make up only one quarter of a complete set of twelve monstrous etudes in all of the minor keys.

Beethoven's Triple Concerto features violin, cello, and piano, and is one of his most unjustly neglected works. Not only is it hard to get three soloists together, but the piece itself has a somewhat experimental feel to it. The problem is that in a sonata-style concerto with three soloists, everything has to get said three or four times. This makes for a very long exposition and not much space for development, which was Beethoven's strong suit. The musical material is lovely, however, even if Bach's rhetorical, polyphonic manner allows his three characters to discuss matters simultaneously from the start, thus saving time.

GROUP 81
A. Scarlatti: *Sonatas (ca. 1738)*
B. Rameau: *Suite for Harpsichord in A minor (1728)*
1. Granados: *Spanish Dances (1892–1900)*
2. Debussy: *Images (Book I) (1905)*
AB A1 B2

Scarlatti composed 555 sonatas for his Spanish and Portuguese patrons, and any collection of them will demonstrate his effervescent sense of fun, as well as his delightful use of characterful Spanish rhythms and harmonies. These single-movement pieces tend to make their best effect on the harpsichord, and they are all relatively brief (about five minutes or so). Try finding a compilation that includes one or several of the following: K. 406, K. 113, K. 518, K. 175, K. 33, K. 444. These are some of the most Spanish-sounding. (Beware: the Scarlatti Sonatas come in both "K"—Kirkpatrick—and "L"—Longo—numbers, though the "K" system is most commonly in use. Check to be sure you're getting the right ones.) It may help to first listen to the Spanish Dances of Granados. Many of the same sounds evident in Scarlatti appear in more concentrated form in Granados. Compare especially the sonata K. 33 with Spanish Dance No. 8. But by all means do make the acquaintance of this wonderfully fresh Baroque master.

Rameau's harpsichord suite, as in any Baroque suite, alternates dance movements with optional character pieces, often with amusing titles (one is called "The Three Hands"). Debussy's first book of *Images* contains as its second movement an "Hommage à Rameau," just as Ravel's *Le tombeau de Couperin* (Group 73) commemorates Rameau's contemporary. Are Debussy's pieces at all aesthetically similar?

GROUP 82
A. Handel: *Israel in Egypt (1739)*
B. Bach: *Mass in B minor (1747–49)*
1. Walton: *Belshazzar's Feast (1931)*
2. Mozart: *Great Mass in C minor (1783)*
AB A1 B2

Handel and Bach are the great choral composers of the Baroque age. Bach composed over two hundred church and secular cantatas, while Handel wrote several dozen operas and oratorios. *Israel in Egypt* and the B-minor Mass represent both composers at their respective peaks, particularly in the writing for chorus.

Israel certainly got around, for by the time Walton wrote his oratorio they had left Egypt for Babylon. Both texts describe God's vengeance on Israel's captors, and Walton's choral writing remains squarely in the grand British tradition inaugurated by Handel, despite the jazz influences. It is definitely one of this century's most exciting pieces in any medium.

All of Mozart's greatest sacred music was destined to remain incomplete. His years in the service of the archbishop of Salzburg were the most miserable in his short life, and most of his other Mass settings do something obnoxious with the text to irritate his patron. Once Mozart left Salzburg, he had little reason to complete any Mass settings. The C-minor Mass, written under the inspiration of his study of the great Baroque masterworks of Handel, thus remained a magnificent torso.

GROUP 83
A. Holst: *The Hymn of Jesus (1917)*
B. Vaughan Williams: *Five Tudor Portraits (1935)*
1. Byrd: *Great Service (ca. 1580)*
2. Orff: *Carmina burana (1936)*
AB A1 B2

Holst and Vaughan Williams represent the sacred and the profane in the British choral tradition. Holst's *Hymn of Jesus* mixes Gregorian chant with the instrumental aura of *The Planets* (Group 33). Vaughan Williams' composition created something of a scandal at its first performance. The racy Elizabethan texts were hardly what the audience expected.

Byrd's Great Service provides a taste of genuine Elizabethan sacred music. Like the Tallis and Palestrina pieces noted in Group 37, Byrd creates a sense of timelessness and religious calm through the medium of unaccompanied chorus, and the lessons of his technique were clearly not lost on Holst.

Orff's *Carmina burana* sets a few naughty lines of its own as it chronicles the life of medieval minstrels and students. The music of the first song became famous through the film *Excalibur,* and it has been a favorite modern choral work since its first performance. Even Barbra Streisand recorded one of its numbers on *Classical Barbra.*

GROUP 84
A. Schmitt: *La tragédie de Salomé (1907)*
B. Strauss: *Salome (1905)*
1. Loeffler: *La mort de Tintagiles (1897)*
2. Zemlinsky: *The Birthday of the Infanta (1922)*
AB A1 B2

The story of Salome, the Judean princess who got John the Baptist's head on a silver platter, has prompted some lusciously decadent music. Schmitt's setting of the tale is a symphonic poem that can also be staged as a ballet. Richard Strauss' opera uses a German translation of Oscar Wilde's French play. For those who can't stomach the whole opera (one act less than two hours long), the famous Dance of the Seven Veils will do, and makes an instructive comparison with the Schmitt.

Loeffler's avowedly decadent tone poem precedes the Schmitt, but still shows many aesthetic similarities despite its paler instrumental colors and less noisy basic framework. If you're into languorous late Romantic sleaze (and who isn't?), it's worth a listen. Zemlinsky's one-act opera, like Strauss', takes for its plot an Oscar Wilde story about yet another psychotic princess. It's a wonderful piece, even shorter than Salome and in some ways more disturbing since the character of the dwarf (I told you it was decadent) at least generates some sympathy.

GROUP 85
A. Barry: *The Lion in Winter* (1967)
B. Goldsmith: *The Omen* (1976)
1. Poulenc: *Stabat Mater* (1950)
2. Stravinsky: *Symphony of Psalms* (1930)
AB A1 B2 A2

Nothing threatens the culture snob more than the possibility of his fixation becoming genuinely popular. Composers, performers, and listeners all participate in a conspiracy that unfairly and, more important, ignorantly makes pointless musical distinctions. How many times have you heard a piece of symphonic music dismissed with the words "It sounds like movie music!"? Well, the simple fact is that many of today's finest composers write for the cinema—this is after all incidental music of the type that used to accompany staged drama—and John Barry and Jerry Goldsmith are two of the best.

All of these compositions take Latin texts of a religious or quasi-religious nature. The point here is not to indignantly accuse the film composers of some sort of plagiarism, but to compare all four works as serious pieces of music. Both Goldsmith and Stravinsky treat their texts in an alienating manner, Goldsmith to depict the terror of the Anti-Christ, and Stravinsky to create a cold, impersonal monumentality. Barry and Poulenc evoke their texts in more traditional fashion, yet there are musical similarities: the quiet choral meditations, violent interjections (compare Barry's "Main Title" with Poulenc's second movement), and most significantly, a haunting, feminine quality created by musical representations of the characters of Eleanor of Aquitaine and the Virgin Mary respectively.

Not the least of the cinema's accomplishments, equally in evidence here, has been the effortlessly idiomatic marriage of electronic, synthesized, and acoustic instruments—a project that has baffled most so-called "serious" composers. It may be that the culture elite refuses to give artists such as Hermann, Waxman, Korngold, Newman, Steiner, Elfman, and Elmer Bernstein their due, but there's no reason why you shouldn't. Keep in mind that music comes in two types, good and bad. Considering the preponderance of the latter, no one can afford to despise quality, wherever it's found.

GROUP 86
A. Ravel: *Quartet (1903)*
B. Debussy: *Quartet (1893)*
1. Vaughan-Williams: *Quartet No. 1 in G minor (1908)*
2. Martinů: *Quartet No. 1 (1918)*
ALL

The Debussy and Ravel quartets are so frequently discussed and recorded together that to think of them separately is like imagining chocolate without peanut butter, to paraphrase the old commercial. And yet different they are, despite similarities in the scherzos and the fact that both employ cyclical construction (rather more obviously in the Debussy). Vaughan-Williams wrote his quartet after three months of study with Ravel. Can you tell? Martinů's sounds so much like either French composer (and is in some ways the most purely gorgeous of all) that you'll wish everyone imitated Debussy and Ravel at least once in their careers.

GROUP 87

A. Britten: *Matinées and Soirées Musicales (1936–41)*
B. Respighi: *Ancient Airs and Dances (Suites 1–3)*
(1917–32)
1. Respighi: *La Boutique Fantasque (1919)*
2. Druckman: *Prism (1980)*
AB A1 B2

The twentieth century has provided composers with a major new artistic form: the pastiche transcription. This involves taking some earlier music and filtering it more or less through some modern sensibility in terms of orchestration, harmony, melody, rhythm, or any combination of these. Here are four examples. The Britten works are based on music by Rossini, as is Respighi's *La Boutique Fantasque.* The *Ancient Airs and Dances* take as their source Renaissance music for lute. Druckman's *Prism* does exactly as the title suggests: it distorts three Baroque and Classical pieces, based on the myth of Medea, through a modern musical lens.

GROUP 88

A. Beethoven: *Septet (Violin, Viola, Cello, Bass, Clarinet, Horn, Bassoon) (1800)*

B. Schubert: *Octet (2 Violins, Viola, Cello, Bass, Clarinet, Horn, Bassoon) (1824)*

1. Saint-Saëns: *Septet (2 Violins, Viola, Cello, Bass, Trumpet, Piano) (1881)*

2. Martinů: *Nonet (Flute, Oboe, Clarinet, Horn, Bassoon, Violin, Viola, Cello, Bass) (1959)*

ALL

Chamber music for lots of instruments starts to get close to orchestral music, and large ensembles such as these rarely call forth from composers their most intense and formally terse works. Rather, the multiplicity of instruments allows for extra movements, colorful musical combinations, and a relaxed atmosphere of charm and fun. And that's exactly what we get.

Glossary

This glossary provides a way to refresh your memory concerning a few frequently used musical terms. Several good dictionaries of musical terms are available, and acquiring one might not be a bad idea. Unfortunately, much of the terminology of music occurs in languages other than English, though the basic list outlined below should provide a decent enough foundation.

adagio: tempo designation meaning "slow," but also a descriptive term for a movement having a solemn and elevated spiritual quality, the classic example being the slow third movement of Beethoven's Ninth Symphony.

allegro: tempo designation meaning "quick."

allegretto: tempo designation for a speed somewhere between andante and allegro.

andante: tempo designation meaning "at a walking pace."

Baroque period: in music, the period extending roughly from the premiere of Monteverdi's opera *Orfeo* in 1607 through the death of Handel in 1759. Its principal innovation was the development of the continuo, the aria (which led to the instrumental concerto), and opera.

canon: a round, such as "Row, Row, Row Your Boat."

cantata: a brief vocal work for any number of voices and instruments unified by subject, but without a narrative plot. Most cantatas alternate arias with recitatives and choruses, and many have a religious theme. The champion cantata composer is Bach, whose works in this form number well over two hundred.

chamber music: music for small forces meant to be played in an intimate setting. After the Baroque, chamber music implies a unique independence of the participating instruments, each of which is both soloist and accompanist. Many of the most important musical innovations occur in this medium and it's very important not to assume that because the instrumental forces are small, the form is small, too. In fact, the opposite is often the case.

chorale: a solemn piece in rich, close harmony, either based on a hymn tune or having a marked religious character. Most of Bach's cantatas end with chorales for the church congregation to sing. To hear a chorale in action, listen to the opening of Wagner's overture to *Tannhäuser,* or to the opening of Bruckner's Fifth Symphony.

Classical period: in music, the period extending roughly from Haydn's early maturity at the end of the Baroque (1759) to the death of Beethoven in 1827. This period was marked by musical composition of a quality that has in many ways never been surpassed. Its great innovations were the establishment of key as the basis of a new, dramatic musical form (sonata form), and the consequent abandonment of the continuo. This led to new ways of treating instruments both singly and in groups.

coda: a musical "tail" or caboose wrapping up a movement. Codas can be either very brief, as are most of Mozart's, or extremely long and developmental, as are many by Haydn and Beethoven.

concertante: not quite a concerto. A work or movement featuring a prominent solo part that does not quite dominate the musical discourse the way a true concerto soloist would. The classic example of this type of writing is the solo viola in Berlioz's *Harold in Italy.*

concerto: a musical composition, usually in several movements or sections, that features a soloist in opposition to the larger orchestra.

continuo: basically, an improvised accompaniment to any number of independent instrumental or vocal musical voices. The development and omnipresence of the continuo was a major characteristic of Baroque music. The most popular continuo instruments are harpsichord, organ, lute, and guitar, with a cello often helping with the bottom-most (bass) line.

contrapuntal: describes a musical texture that consists of "polyphony"; two or more independent voices. Counterpoint is the set of rules governing the writing of polyphonic music. It's a feature of all musical periods and varieties of composition.

development: most musical compositions indulge in this, but it has a specific meaning in terms of sonata form, being the section that initiates the struggle to return to the tonic, or home key.

Dies irae: "Day of Wrath"—the text depicting the horrors of Judgment Day from the Catholic Mass for the Dead (Requiem). Liszt's *Totentanz* is based on the famous Gregorian chant tune, as is the finale of Berlioz's *Symphony fantastique,* and just about anything by Rachmaninoff. Most composers who didn't actually quote the ancient tune note for note at least set the text in their own Requiems.

episode: in general, any musical section that can be marked off from any other, but specifically, in a fugue, any point at which the main theme, or subject, of the fugue is not present.

exposition: in sonata form, the initial presentation of the thematic material of the movement. In a fugue, the recurring presentation of the subject.

fantasia: a musical composition in more or less free form; also a film by Walt Disney.

finale: the last movement or section of any multimovement work.

fugue: a contrapuntal style similar to that of a canon, or round, except that the tune (or subject) enters on successively different notes of the scale. One of the most important contrapuntal techniques.

grave: tempo designation for "very, very slow."

homophonic: a musical texture consisting of a tune with a simple accompaniment. The opening of Mozart's Symphony No. 40 is a good example.

key: one of twenty-four possible musical locations in our harmonic system, any one of which can function as a sort of musical home base.

largo: tempo designation for "very slow."

lento: tempo designation somewhere between andante and adagio, rather slow.

major: the basic, most stable form of the scale based on any of the twelve available notes, usually having a happy or contented emotional quality.

minor: the alternative, less stable versions of the scale based on any of the twelve available notes (thus twenty-four possible keys, including both major and minor). Music in minor keys tends to have unhappy or tense emotional qualities.

minuet: a dance in triple time that was a precursor to the waltz. Most Baroque orchestral suites included one, and it became the only surviving dance movement in Classical symphonies and chamber music before it was supplanted by the scherzo.

moderato: tempo designation that is self-explanatory—moderate.

Modern: musically speaking, the period where we are now, succeeding the Romantic and beginning with the death of Mahler in 1911. The term has no stylistic significance, because we are too close to the preceding eighty-odd years to see what the next generations will make of them—or us.

opus: work. A means of designating, via the "opus number," a particular musical composition.

oratorio: a large-scale work for singers and instruments that has a clear narrative thread. The oratorio tradition was most popular in England with the works of Handel, though many other composers from Bach to Haydn and Elgar and Mendelssohn composed in this form.

ostinato: an "obstinate" rhythmic or melodic pattern that repeats itself over and over. The classic example is Ravel's *Boléro,* though Janáček, Sibelius, and Bruckner all loved to use ostinatos as a means of musical propulsion.

overture: obviously first and foremost a curtain-raiser to a play or opera, but also a suite of orchestral movements consisting (in the Baroque) of a large and impressive polyphonic introduction followed by a selection of lighter dances. The term persisted well into the Classical period, with many of what we now call symphonies originally designated as overtures.

passacaglia: a series of variations over a repeating bass line. The most famous orchestral example is the finale of Brahms' Fourth Symphony, though the form is very popular with modern composers such as Britten, Shostakovich, and Tippett.

pathétique: not "pathetic," but dramatic and moody. Nickname of Beethoven's Eighth Piano Sonata, and Tchaikovsky's last symphony.

pentatonic: a scale having only five notes, corresponding to the black keys on our piano, characteristic of much Oriental and folk music. The opening of Dvořák's "American" Quartet is a pentatonic tune.

polyphonic: "many voices." Music in two or more independent lines written in contrapuntal style, meaning that the various lines retain their musical identities and play off against each other.

prelude: a short introduction, but in the hands of Chopin and later keyboard composers an independent but brief musical mood picture.

presto: tempo designation for "very fast."

programmatic: music having a descriptive purpose in addition to its purely musical objectives.

recapitulation: in sonata form, the restatement of the material of the exposition after the development section, and the moment at which the home key, or tonic, is reestablished.

recitative: sung speech. Dialogue which is set to music to bridge the gaps and hurry the plot along in opera or oratorio, and lead into the arias. In Baroque and Classical music, most recitative is very lightly accompanied by just piano or harpsichord, and is thus called "secco," or "dry" recitative. When recitative style is used by instruments alone (as in the opening of the finale of Beethoven's Ninth), the effect is heavily rhetorical.

Renaissance: in music, the Renaissance is somewhat out of phase with the actual, historical Renaissance, largely consisting of works composed during the Reformation and Counter-Reformation in the latter half of the sixteenth century. The highest products of this period are Mass settings for unaccompanied choir by composers such as Palestrina, Victoria, Lassus, and Byrd.

Requiem: the Latin Mass for the Dead.

ritornello: in a concerto, the initial statement by the orchestra of the thematic material of the first movement, which will return at various points as a unifying element. Also, in a rondo, the recurring tune that separates the various episodes.

Romantic period: in music, the period extending roughly from Beethoven's middle period (1805) to the death of Mahler in 1911. This end date is highly suspect, since the highly emotional, orchestrally brilliant Romantic style is certainly still with us. It may be that we haven't run out of romance quite yet.

rondo: a movement, often a finale, having the form ABACADA, etc.

scherzo: literally "joke," the dance movement that replaced the minuet in Classical and Romantic instrumental music. A scherzo is often quite a bit faster than the old minuet.

sinfonia: very similar to the overture, though usually following the fast-slow-fast format as opposed to the French overture's slow-fast-slow.

sonata: a word that has meant different things at different times. Generally, a sonata is a composition in several movements or sections for one or two instruments, anything larger having another name, such as trio. In the Classical era, the organization of large forms around the dramatic conflict of various key areas came to be called "sonata form," and this sense is still the most significant today.

Sturm und Drang: "storm and stress." Describes highly emotional, tense music in minor keys, such as that of Haydn's middle period in the 1760s.

subject: as the term implies, the object of a musical discourse consisting in a fugue of the principal theme, and in a sonata movement of several themes or groups of themes in different key areas.

symphony: a composition for orchestra, usually divided into four major sections called movements.

trio: obviously a composition for three instruments or parts, but also the central section of a dance or march movement in ABA form. The famous "graduation theme" from Elgar's "Pomp and Circumstance" March No. 1 is a trio.

variation: in essence, taking a tune and playing with it, changing melody, harmony, or accompaniment. One of the very basic principles of musical form.

Index of Musical Compositions

·

A FINAL NOTE TO THE READER

I'm not sure what exactly it may reveal of my working methods to say so, but compiling this index brought me face to face, for the first time, with a complete list of the music discussed in this book. The experience raises a few thoughts that I'd like to share with you. First of all, there really is a lot of music here (well over five hundred separate pieces, ranging in length from a few minutes to a few hours). It's enough for years of listening, assuming you wish to assimilate all of it. But it's also a drop in the bucket. There's so much more I would have liked to include, and I'm sure that even the minimally experienced will know of something that, frustratingly, isn't here. After all, why include all of Beethoven's symphonies except for the First and *my* personal favorite, the Fourth? All I can say is that it just worked out that way. True, I can always make up more listening groups, and perhaps I'll have the chance; but the line had to be drawn somewhere, and I wanted above all a book of sensible length.

The thought occurs to me, however, that just because my list is manageable, you still have to go to your local record emporium and face down zillions of recordings by people you may never have heard of. There's really not much to be done about this most physically intimidating aspect of our musical heritage. It *is* vast, and the sooner this expanse ignites in you the enthusiasm of the explorer, the quicker the thrill of discovery will supplant the daunting prospect of having to conquer so much territory.

Another reason that the musical thicket seems so impenetrable may have something to do with the extremely varied, elaborate, unscientific, even irrational means employed in identifying musical works (as discussed a bit in the chapter on buying recordings). This I *can* do something about. I have emphasized, in making this index, the need to have only the barest minimum of information necessary for correct identification of the piece in question. My aim throughout has been essentially pragmatic. Thus, some entries under the same composer will include identifiers such as opus numbers or key signatures, while others will not, depending on the necessity.

Some entries may deviate slightly in form from the titles given in the body of the book. The fact is, however unscholarly it may be, details such as word order rarely matter in practice, as long as the words chosen are the right ones. The secret in getting around the repertoire does not lie in memorizing quantities of tedious detail—it's in knowing what single piece of information is most important. This experience will come in time, but I think it helps to have firsthand exposure to the variety of possible accurate descriptions and titles, as long as this does not complicate matters further (and it shouldn't here).

Names and dates are taken, for the most part, from the *New Grove Dictionary of Music and Musicians*, though I have not adopted its spellings where I believe they contradict common usage (as they frequently do in Russian music, for instance).

I have placed in italics works which occur in *both* Parts One and Two. These pieces make excellent places to start listening. My purpose in adopting this colloquial method is both to simplify your search, and at the same time to suggest subtly that you pay attention to what you see as well as to what you hear. As I've said before: a little time, a little thought, and there are no limits to the possible rewards.

Alkan, Charles-Valentin (1813–1888; French):
Concerto for Piano Solo 204
Grand Sonate "The Four Ages" 189
Alwyn, William (1905–1985; English):
Fantasy Waltzes 190

Bach, Johann Sebastian (1685–1750; German):
B minor Mass 206
Brandenburg Concertos 137
Concerto No. 1 in D minor for Harpsichord and Orchestra, BWV 1052 153
Concerto in C major for Two Harpsichords, BWV 1061 174
Concerto in C minor for Two Harpsichords, BWV 1062 174
Concerto for Four Harpsichords 174
Concerto in D minor for Two Violins 174
Fantasy and Fugue in C minor for Organ, BWV 537 193
Goldberg Variations 197
Inventions (Two- and Three-Part) 185
Italian Concerto 204
Overtures (Orchestral Suites) 145
Triple Concerto, BWV 1044 204
Barber, Samuel (1910–1981; American):
Violin Concerto 102, 103
Barry, John (1933– ; English composer of film music):
The Lion in Winter 209
Bartók, Béla (1881–1945; Hungarian):
Concerto for Orchestra 164
Dance Suite 138
Divertimento for Strings 132
The Miraculous Mandarin 169
Music for Strings, Percussion and Celesta 171
Piano Concerto No. 2 103
String Quartet No. 6 198
Bax, Arnold (1883–1953; English):
Symphony No. 2 160
Tintagel 110, 167
Beethoven, Ludwig van (1770–1827; German):
Diabelli Variations 197
"Kreutzer" Sonata (Violin Sonata No. 9) 192
Leonore Overture No. 3 141
Missa Solemnis 201
"Moonlight" Sonata 188

"Pathétique" Sonata 196
Piano Concerto No. 5 "Emperor" 158
Piano Sonata No. 21 "Waldstein" 187
Quintet for Piano and Winds, op. 16 183
"Rasumovsky" Quartet No. 1 (String Quartet No. 7 in F) 192
Septet 212
String Quartet No. 14 in C-sharp minor, op. 131 90
Symphony No. 2 149
Symphony No. 3 "Eroica" 54
Symphony No. 5 135
Symphony No. 6 "Pastorale" 140, 141
Symphony No. 7 135
Symphony No. 8 179
Symphony No. 9 "Choral" 150
Triple Concerto 204
Violin Concerto 100
Berg, Alban (1885–1935; Austrian):
Violin Concerto 103
Three Pieces for Orchestra 147
Berio, Luciano (1925– ; Italian):
Sinfonia 151
Berlioz, Hector (1803–1869; French):
The Damnation of Faust 168
Harold in Italy 112, 175
Les nuits d'été 172
Romeo and Juliet 108
Symphonie Fantastique 112, 140
Bernstein, Leonard (1918–1990; American):
"Candide" Overture 141
Symphony No. 2 "The Age of Anxiety" 175
West Side Story 108
Berwald, Franz (1796–1868; Swedish):
Symphonie Singuliere 175
Bizet, Georges (1838–1875; French):
Carmen (Suite) 166
Bloch, Ernest (1880–1959; Swiss):
Schelomo 119
Violin Sonata No. 1 200
Violin Sonata No. 2 "Poème Mystique" 184
Borodin, Alexander (1833–1887; Russian):
String Quartet No. 2 186
Brahms, Johannes (1833–1897; German):
Clarinet Quintet 182
Clarinet Sonata No. 1 in F minor 182
German Requiem 202
Paganini Variations (Books I and II) 195
Piano Concerto No. 1 158
Piano Quartet No. 1 in G minor 193

Piano Quintet in F minor 184
Piano Trio in C minor 180
Symphony No. 1 135
Symphony No. 2 152
Symphony No. 3 163
Symphony No. 4 60, 139, 140
Variations on a Theme by Haydn 72
Violin Concerto 101
Brian, Havergal (1876–1972; English):
Gothic Symphony 168
Bridge, Frank (1879–1941; English):
Piano Trio No. 2 191
The Sea 110
Suite for String Orchestra 171
Britten, Benjamin (1913–1976; English):
*Four Sea Interludes from "Peter
Grimes"* 110, 138
Matinées and Soirées Musicales 211
The Turn of the Screw 172, 173
Variations on a Theme by Frank
Bridge 171
War Requiem 202
The Young Person's Guide to the
Orchestra 71
Bruch, Max (1838–1920; German).
Violin Concerto No. 1 in G minor 101
Bruckner, Anton (1824–1896; Austrian):
String Quintet 194
Symphony No. 4 "Romantic" 139, 140
Symphony No. 5 121
Symphony No. 7 176
Symphony No. 8 146
Symphony No. 9 163
Te Deum 201
Byrd, William (1543–1623; English):
The Great Service 207

Chausson, Ernest (1855–1899; French):
Piano Trio in G minor 180
Symphony in B-flat 173
Chávez, Carlos (1899–1978; Mexican):
Sinfonia India 171, 172
Cherubini, Luigi (1760–1842; Italian):
Coronation Mass 203
Chopin, Frédéric (1810–1849; Polish):
Etudes 185
Piano Sonata No. 2 189
Preludes (24) 190
Waltzes 190
Clarke, Rebecca (1886–1979; English):
Piano Trio 191
Copland, Aaron (1900–1990; American):

Appalachian Spring 136
Short Symphony 146
Symphony No. 3 178
Couperin, François (1668–1733; French):
Suite for Harpsichord No 11 (from Book
II) 197

Debussy, Claude (1862–1918; French):
Etudes 185
Ibéria (Images for Orchestra No. 2) 166
Images for Piano (Book I) 205
La Mer 110
Nocturnes 148, 149
Piano Trio in G major 186, 187
Préludes for Piano (Books I and II) 190
Quartet 210
Trio for Flute, Harp and Viola 186, 187
Violin Sonata 181
Delius, Frederick (1862–1934; English):
Sea Drift 156
Dohnányi, Ernst von (1877–1960;
Hungarian):
Piano Quintet in C minor 184, 185
Serenade for String Trio 199
Sextet for Piano, Horn, Clarinet, and
String Trio 184, 185
Variations on a Nursery Tune 195
Druckman, Jacob (1928– ; American):
Aureole 111
Prism 211
Dukas, Paul (1865–1935; French):
La Péri 159, 160
Symphony in C 173
Dutilleux, Henri (1916– ; French):
Metaboles 74
Dvořák, Antonin (1841–1904; Czech):
"American" Quartet (String Quartet
No. 12) 194
Cello Concerto 101
Piano Trio in F minor, op. 65 88, 180
String Quartet No. 10 in E-flat 186
String Quintet in E-flat, op. 97 194
Symphonic Variations 72
Symphony No. 6 152
Symphony No. 7 in D minor 88, 139, 140
Symphony No. 8 155
Symphony No. 9 "From the New
World" 148
Serenade for Strings 132
Serenade for Winds 132
Slavonic Dances 138
The Water Goblin 110

Elgar, Edward (1857–1934; English):
Enigma Variations 73
In the South 167
Introduction and Allegro 171
Pomp and Circumstance Marches 137
Symphony No. 2 160
Violin Concerto 102
Enescu, George (1881–1955; Rumanian):
Orchestral Suites 145

Falla, Manuel de (1876–1946; Spanish):
El Amor Brujo 110
Nights in the Gardens of Spain 148, 149
The Three-Cornered Hat 144
Fauré, Gabriel (1845–1924; French):
Piano Quintet No. 1 in D minor 184, 185
Violin Sonata No. 1 in A 192
Violin Sonata No. 2 181
Franck, César (1822–1890; French):
Symphony in D minor 176
Violin Sonata 181

Gershwin, George (1898–1937; American):
Rhapsody in Blue 139
Goldmark, Karl (1830–1915; Hungarian):
Rustic Wedding Symphony 136
Goldsmith, Jerry (1929– ; American film composer):
The Omen (Part 1) 209
Granados, Enrique (1867–1916; Spanish):
Spanish Dances 205
Grieg, Edvard (1843–1907; Norwegian):
Peer Gynt Suite No. 1 (but the more extended selections are well worth having) 111
Grofé, Ferde (1892–1972; American):
Grand Canyon Suite 111, 161

Handel, George Frideric (1685–1759; English):
Israel in Egypt 206
Royal Fireworks Music 149
Water Music 136
Hanson, Howard (1896–1981; American):
Romantic Symphony (Symphony No. 2) 167
Harris, Roy (1898–1979; American):
Symphony No. 3 178
Haydn, Joseph (1732–1809; Austrian):
The Creation 111
Lord Nelson Mass 203

Mass in Time of War 201
Piano Sonata in C minor (No. 33) 196
Piano Sonata in E-flat (Hoboken No. 52, Landon No. 62) 187
String Quartet in E-flat, op. 33 No. 2 "Joke" 187
String Quartet in C major, op. 54 No. 2 198
String Quartet in F major, op. 74 No. 2 198
String Quartet in C, op. 76 No. 3 "Emperor" 83
Symphony No. 44 "Mourning" 196
Symphony No. 45 "Farewell" 163
Symphony No. 88 50
Symphony No. 93 179
Symphony No. 94 "Surprise" 83
Symphony No. 100 "Military" 156
Symphony No. 102 102
Symphony No. 103 "Drumroll" 150
Symphony No. 104 "London" 149
Te Deum in C (1800) 201
Hindemith, Paul (1895–1963; German):
Mathis der Maler (Symphony) 133, 151
Nobilissima Visione 139
Requiem 202
Symphonic Metamorphosis of Themes by Carl Maria von Weber 137
Symphony in E-flat 157
Holst, Gustav (1874–1934; English):
Ballet Music from "The Perfect Fool" 110
Choral Symphony 112
The Hymn of Jesus 207
The Planets 114, 161
Savitri 172
Honegger, Arthur (1892–1955; Swiss):
Pacific 231 108
Symphony No. 1 200
Symphony No. 3 "Liturgique" 142

Ives, Charles (1874–1954; American):
Symphony No. 4 151
Three Places in New England 171, 172

Janáček, Léoš (1854–1928; Czech):
Mladi (*see* Youth)
Glagolitic Mass 203
Sinfonietta 120, 121, 146
String Quartet No. 1 "Kreutzer Sonata" 192
String Quartet No. 2 "Intimate Pages" 194

Taras Bulba   155
Youth (Wind Sextet)   132

Kodály, Zoltan (1882–1967; Hungarian):
Serenade for Two Violins and Viola   199
Koechlin, Charles (1867–1950; French):
Quintette Primavera for Flute, Harp and
    String Trio   186, 187
Kokkonen, Joonas (1921– ; Finnish):
Symphony No. 4   157

Liszt, Franz (1811–1886; Hungarian):
Dante Symphony   110
Sonata in B minor   188
Totentanz   69, 138
Loeffler, Charles Martin (1861–1935;
    American):
La Mort de Tintagiles   208
Lutoslawski, Witold (1913– ; Polish):
Symphony No. 3   124

Magnard, Albéric (1865–1914; French):
Quintet for Piano and Winds   183
Symphony No. 4   176
Violin Sonata   181
Mahler, Gustav (1860–1911; Austrian):
Das Lied von der Erde   159
Kindertotenlieder   172
Symphony No. 1   140
Symphony No. 2 "Resurrection"   150
Symphony No. 3   137
Symphony No. 4   179
Symphony No. 5   156
Symphony No. 6   147
Symphony No. 7   164
Symphony No. 8   168
Symphony No. 9   177
Martin, Frank (1890–1974; Swiss):
Petite Symphonie Concertante   157
Martinů, Bohuslav (1890–1959; Czech):
Double Concerto for Two String
    Orchestras, Piano and Timpani 171, 172
The Frescoes of Pierro della Francesca 133
Nonet   212
Piano Quintet No. 2   191
Quartet No. 1   210
Symphony No. 4   178
Mendelssohn, Felix (1809–1847; German):
The Hebrides (Fingal's Cave) Overture 110
Italian Symphony (Symphony No. 4) 175
Violin Concerto in E minor, op. 64   100

Messaien, Olivier (1908– ; French):
Turangalîla-Symphonie   164
Milhaud, Darius (1892–1974; French):
The Creation of the World   139
Moeran, E. J. (1894–1950; English):
String Quartet   186
Symphony in G minor   160
Monteverdi, Claudio (1567–1643; Italian):
Combattimento di Tancredi e Clorinda 118
Mozart, Wolfgang Amadeus (1756–1791;
    Austrian):
Clarinet Quintet   182
Eine Kleine Nachtmusik   46, 47
Fantasia in C minor (for Piano)   188
Great Mass in C minor   206
Piano Concerto No. 20 in D minor   96
Piano Concerto No. 21   153
Quintet for Piano and Winds K. 452 183
String Quartet in D minor, K. 421   195
String Quintet in E-flat, K. 614   195
Symphony No. 38 "Prague"   153
Symphony No. 40 in G minor   134
Symphony No. 41 "Jupiter"   149
Variations on "Ah, vous dirai-je,
    Maman"   195
Mussorgsky, Modest (1839–1881; Russian):
Pictures at an Exhibition (orch. Ravel) 161

Nielsen, Carl (1865–1931; Danish):
Clarinet Concerto   102
Symphony No. 3 "Espansiva"   158
Symphony No. 4 "The
    Inextinguishable"   153, 154
Symphony No. 5   177
Novák, Vitězslav (1870–1949; Czech):
Piano Trio in D minor   180

Orff, Carl (1895–1982; German):
Carmina Burana   207

Palestrina, Giovanni Pierluigi da (ca. 1525–
    1594, Italian):
Pope Marcellus Mass (Missa Papae
    Marcelli)   165
Piston, Walter (1894–1976; American):
Symphony No. 6   178
Poulenc, Francis (1899–1963; French):
Clarinet Sonata   182
Concert Champêtre for Harpsichord and
    Orchestra   153
Stabat Mater   209

Trio for Piano, Oboe, and Bassoon 187
Prokofiev, Sergei (1891–1953; Russian):
Classical Symphony 134
Romeo and Juliet 108
Scythian Suite 169
Symphony No. 5 170
Symphony No. 6 142

Rachmaninoff, Sergei (1873–1943; Russian):
The Isle of the Dead 162
Piano Concerto No. 2 101
Piano Sonata No. 1 in D minor 189
Rhapsody on a Theme by Paganini 70
Symphony No. 1 170
Symphonic Dances 138
Rameau, Jean-Philippe (1683–1764; French):
Suite for Harpsichord in A minor 205
Ravel, Maurice (1875–1937; French):
Boléro 69
Daphnis and Chloé 112, 177
Introduction and Allegro 199
La Valse 148
Le Tombeau de Couperin 197
Mother Goose (Ma Mère l'Oye) 143
Piano Concerto for the Left Hand 139
Piano Concerto in G 153
Piano Trio 186
Quartet 210
Rhapsodie Espagnol 166
Schéhérazade 159
Respighi, Ottorino (1879–1936; Italian):
Ancient Airs and Dances (Suites 1–3) 211
Church Windows 133
The Fountains of Rome 110, 161
La Boutique Fantasque 211
The Pines of Rome 161
Roman Festivals 161
Rimsky-Korsakov, Nicolai (1844–1908; Russian):
Capriccio Espagnol 166
Schéhérazade 110
Rossini, Gioachino (1792–1868; Italian):
"The Barber of Seville" Overture 141
"The Thieving Magpie" Overture 154
Roussel, Albert (1869–1937; French):
Bacchus and Ariadne 177
Serenade for Flute, Harp, and String Trio 199
Symphony No. 2 173
Symphony No. 3 146
Ruggles, Carl (1876–1971; American):
Sun Treader 111

Saint-Saëns, Camille (1835–1921; French):
Bacchanale from "Samson and Delilah" 112, 143
Danse Macabre 148
Septet 212
Symphony No. 3 "Organ" 173
Scarlatti, Domenico (1685–1757; Italian):
Sonatas 205
Schmitt, Florent (1870–1958; French):
La Tragédie de Salomé 208
Schoenberg, Arnold (1874–1951; Austrian):
Chamber Symphony No. 1 144
Gurrelieder 168
Pierrot Lunaire 162
Suite for Strings in G 145
Verklärte Nacht (Transfigured Night) 152
Schrecker, Franz (1878–1934; Austrian):
Chamber Symphony 144
Schubert, Franz (1797–1828; Austrian):
Octet 212
Piano Trio No. 1 in B-flat 198
String Quartet No. 14 in D minor "Death and the Maiden" 195
String Quintet in C major, D. 956 195
Symphony No. 5 134
Symphony No. 8 "Unfinished" 163
Symphony No. 9 "The Great" 150
"Wanderer" Fantasie 188
Schumann, Robert (1810–1856; German):
Piano Concerto 158
Symphonic Etudes 185
Symphony No. 3 "Rhenish" 140
Symphony No. 4 153, 154
Scriabin, Alexander (1872–1915; Russian):
Poem of Ecstasy 184
Symphony No. 2 154
Shapero, Harold (1920– ; American):
Symphony for Classical Orchestra 200
Shostakovich, Dmitri (1906–1975; Russian):
Piano Trio No. 2, op. 67 191
Symphony No. 5 151
Symphony No. 8 142
Symphony No. 9 179
Symphony No. 10 170
Sibelius, Jean (1865–1957; Finnish):
The Oceanides 110
Pohjola's Daughter 120
Symphony No. 3 176
Symphony No. 4 147
Symphony No. 5 153, 154
Symphony No. 6 165
Symphony No. 7 158, 159

Tapiola 119, 120
Violin Concerto 102
Smetana, Bedrich (1824–1884; Czech):
Má Vlast (My Country) 155
String Quartet No. 1 "From My Life" 186
Sousa, John Philip (1854–1932; American):
Marches 137
Stenhammar, Wilhelm (1871–1927; Swedish):
Symphony No. 2 158
Strauss Jr., Johann (1825–1899; Austrian):
Waltzes 148
Strauss, Richard (1864–1949; German):
Also Sprach Zarathustra 111, 148
Death and Transfiguration 196
Don Juan 167
Salome 208
Stravinsky, Igor (1882–1971; Russian):
Dumbarton Oaks 137, 138
The Firebird (Suite) 164
Pétrouchka 144
Pulcinella 137, 138
The Rite of Spring 169
Symphony in Three Movements 157
Symphony of Psalms 209
Suk, Josef (1874–1935; Czech):
A Summer Tale 155
Szymanowski, Karol (1882–1937; Polish):
Myths for Violin and Piano 184

Tallis, Thomas (ca. 1505–1585; English):
Spem in Alium 118, 165
Tchaikovsky, Peter Ilyich (1840–1893; Russian):
Francesca da Rimini 111, 162
Manfred Symphony 112, 113
Romeo and Juliet 108
Symphony No. 4 135
Symphony No. 6 "Pathétique" 170
Thuille, Ludwig (1861–1907; Austrian):
Sextet for Piano and Winds, op. 6 183
Tippett, Michael (1905– ; English):
Concerto for Double String Orchestra 171
Ritual Dances from "The Midsummer Marriage" 110, 111
Symphony No. 1 200
Tubin, Eduard (1905–1982; Estonian):
Symphony No. 2 "Legendary" 158

Varèse, Edgard (1883–1965; American):
Amériques 169

Vaughan Williams, Ralph (1872–1958; English):
Fantasia on a Theme by Thomas Tallis 165
Five Tudor Portraits 207
Job 133
A London Symphony (Symphony No. 2) 148
A Pastoral Symphony (Symphony No. 3) 160
Quartet No. 1 in G minor 210
A Sea Symphony (Symphony No. 1) 156
Sinfonia Antartica (Symphony No. 7) 114
Symphony No. 6 142
Verdi, Giuseppe (1813–1901; Italian):
Aida 143
Requiem 202
Villa-Lobos, Heitor (1887–1959; Brazilian):
Bacchianas Brasileiras No. 2 108
Quintet for Flute, Harp and String Trio 184
Vivaldi, Antonio (1678–1741; Italian):
Concerto for Four Violins, op. 3 No. 10 174
The Four Seasons 31, 137

Wagner, Richard (1813–1883; German):
Prelude and Liebestod from "Tristan and Isolde" 152
"Rienzi" Overture 154
Der Ring des Nibelungen (Orchestral Excerpts) 110, 154, 155
Venusberg Ballet from "Tannhäuser" 112, 143
Walton, William (1902–1983; English):
Belshazzar's Feast 206
Coronation Te Deum 203
Façade 162
Symphony No. 1 147
Variations on a Theme by Hindemith 73, 74
Weber, Carl Maria von (1786–1826; German):
"Der Freischütz" Overture 141
Konzertstück in F minor for Piano and Orchestra 99, 158
Weill, Kurt (1900–1950; German):
Suite from "The Threepenny Opera" (Kleine Dreigroschenmusik) 139
Williams, John (1932– ; American):
Star Wars 114
Zelenka, Jan Dismas (1679–1745; Czech):
Capriccios 145

Sonatas for Two Oboes and Bassoon   77

Zemlinsky, Alexander von (1871–1942;
    Austrian):

The Birthday of the Infanta
    (The Dwarf)   208

Lyric Symphony   159

About the Author

DAVID HURWITZ works in real estate, is a musician, and has written extensively about music and classical recordings for numerous magazines, such as *High Fidelity* and *Fanfare*. He lives in New York City.